WHEAT SONGS

A Greek-American Journey

Library of Congress Cataloging-in-Publication Data

Names: Rizopoulos, Perry Giuseppe, 1991- author. | Meis, William A., Jr., author.

Title: Wheat songs : a Greek-American journey / Perry Giuseppe Rizopoulos with William A. Meis, Jr. Description: Boston : Cherry Orchard Books, an imprint of Academic Studies Press, 2018. | Includes bibliographical references and index.

Identifiers: LCCN 2018023267 (print) | LCCN 2018034381 (ebook) | ISBN 9781618117731 (ebook) | ISBN 9781618117717 (hardcover : alk. paper) | ISBN 9781618117724 (paperback : alk. paper)

Subjects: LCSH: Rizopoulos, Perry Giuseppe, 1991—Family. | Greek Americans–New York (State)–Bronx County–Biography. | Italian Americans–New York (State)–Bronx County–Biography. | Greece–History–20th century.

Classification: LCC F128.9.G7 (ebook) | LCC F128.9.G7 R59 2018 (print) | DDC 949.507–dc23

LC record available at https://lccn.loc.gov/2018023267

© Academic Studies Press, 2018
ISBN 9781618117717 (hardcover)
ISBN 9781618117724 (paper)

Book design by Kryon Publishing Services (P) Ltd.
www.kryonpublishing.com

Cover design by Ivan Grave

Published by Cherry Orchard Books, an imprint of Academic Studies Press

28 Montfern Avenue
Brighton, MA 02135, USA
press@academicstudiespress.com
www.academicstudiespress.com

WHEAT SONGS

A Greek-American Journey

PERRY GIUSEPPE
RIZOPOULOS

WITH WILLIAM A. MEIS, JR.

Boston
2018

Dedicated to the people and the places that raised me, thank you.

A special thanks to my family, my girlfriend and my friends for your support and love. Also, a special thanks to Dr. Hope Leichter and Dr. Mehnaz Afridi. Your guidance and encouragement are invaluable and were integral for bringing this piece to life. I am forever grateful for all of you.

Table of Contents

CHAPTER 1

Difficult Choices

"What you leave behind is not what is engraved on stone monuments, but what is woven into the lives of others."

—**Pericles, Greek Statesman,**
Orator and General of Athens during the Golden Age.

Pericles Rizopoulos should have died a long time ago, along with his brother, Panayiotis, in the rose limestone mountains of Northern Greece overlooking the blue crystal waters of Lake Orestiada. They faced death from the poisonous fangs of an angry horned viper while the brothers hid beneath the graceful branches of a weeping willow tree. When the viper aggressively stretched itself out and gazed intently at the brothers, they had no choice but to remain completely immobile for as long as possible while the twitching snake decided which brother to strike first. Or, if they ran, there were Nazi soldiers on the other side of the willow's protective branches. The Nazi snakes or the horned viper? A very difficult choice.

But a choice was made because there we sat in his dining room in the Bronx, New York, seventy years after my grandfather's first brush with death with only a few months remaining before his last. As I looked across the table at Pericles, my grandfather's eyes were bright, his hands were scarred but his spirit was strong. Before he was my grandfather, he was a father, a husband, a fighter, a survivor, a Greek, and a young boy facing a vicious and powerful chaos that would have paralyzed most grown men.

Hard choices have been the fate of Greeks during the last 500 years. In earlier times, we were the glorious dawn of Western Civilization—the philosophy of Socrates, Plato and Aristotle, the science of Euclid and Archimedes, the medicine of Hippocrates, the theater of Euripides & Sophocles, the poetry of

Sappho, Homer's *Iliad* and the *Odyssey*, Herodotus' history and the architecture of the Parthenon. And then, in 330, when the Roman emperor Constantine moved his capitol to Greek Byzantium from Latin Rome, there were the glories of the Byzantine Empire, of Κωνσταντινούπολις, Constantinople, now Istanbul, the magnificent Greek city on the Bosporus that controlled the rich trade between Asia and Europe. The Byzantine Empire was the most powerful economic, cultural, and military force in Europe, as well as the cultural and religious heart of Eastern Europe and the Middle East.

Then, in 1453, Constantinople fell to the Turks, and all that had been Greek was overwhelmed by the Ottoman Empire. Since then, we Greeks have been facing obstacles at times created by Turks, Italians, Germans, French, British and even Americans. We have always fought back. We have always fought for the freedom and democracy that were the founding ideals of ancient Greece.

But we have also, just as we did in the ancient Peloponnesian Wars when Sparta and Athens became bitter rivals, fought with each other. Unfortunately, we are still fighting with each other. Hard choices. These hard choices however, have often made us into very resilient people. Just as in Albert Camus' portrayal of Sisyphus whose face pressed so close to stone became like stone, so too have Greeks gained strength from their difficulties. Pericles Rizopoulos was παππούς μου, my *pappou*, my grandfather and he was one of these strong people.

Looking back, I recall that the most important meeting I had with him was when I was just eleven years old. It was a hot, sticky, New York summer morning when I stopped by to visit with him on my way home from my cousin's house. I had only just walked in the door when my grandfather told me that I should sit at the dining room of the dimly lit first floor of their home in the Bronx, New York. His and Mollie's house. Mollie was η γιαγιά μου, my *yiayia*, my grandmother.

My pappou was an old man even then, but on that day he was expectant, vigorous and excited. He sat down next to me and showed me a red covered, bound, unlined book that he handled with such respect, such reverence, that even before he told me what the book was, I intuitively understood that this was a very important document. He sat down and stared at me. "Perrymou," he said, "this book is the key to my life…and to your life. It is a story about φιλότιμο (*philotimo*)."

We sat on the couch where the sun came through the blinds, reflected light onto the book and illuminated pappou's gold crucifix that hung from his neck. The house was unbearably warm. Using their air conditioning was always viewed as a sign of weakness and a waste of money, so we both sat in our undershirts and tirelessly went through every page of the book. As he carefully folded back the pages and translated the handwritten Greek, I was totally captivated by his stories of war, adventure and survival, and he was unrelenting in his telling. We spent the whole day together, without a break, just the two of us. He never stopped speaking, and I never stopped listening.

Ten years after our first conversation, in September 2013, when I was 21 years old, I was sitting in a classroom on my first day of graduate school at Columbia University's Teachers College. The class was called "Family as Educator," and my professor, Dr. Hope Jensen Leichter, Director of the Elbenwood Center for the Study of Family as Educator, waited for class to begin and walked up to each and every student, shook each student's hand and asked how we were doing. After these brief conversations, she walked to the front of the room and asked the class to share a story that showed how our grandparents educated us. I sat in the middle of the room and listened attentively to each student when I suddenly found myself reflecting on that remarkable day I spent with my grandfather. It was my turn to speak and Dr. Leichter looked at me with an expectant smile as I shared the bits of the story that I could remember. I felt the importance of that experience growing with each example I provided.

At that time, pappou could still go outside and work in his yard, cook and walk around freely. Yet, I sensed that he was getting weaker. At family gatherings he was quieter, less responsive.

But the others in my family preferred not to focus on pappou's warning signs. My father refused to say or do anything but encourage pappou while convincing himself that his father was going to make a 180 degree turn and be completely healthy again. Yiayia Mollie, my grandmother, was also becoming somewhat forgetful and absent-minded. Then there was my mother. She noticed, but also did not want to exacerbate the obvious. I did not want to look away from what my pappou was saying and what he was doing. When I told our story to my class, I faced the reality.

That's when it occurred to me that I should go to see pappou and find that notebook. I decided my grandfather and I would read through his brother's journal, and he would tell me their stories while he was still able to do so. We'd be together... again, like we were on that distant summer morning.

A few days later, when I was in the Bronx, I stopped by my pappou's house unannounced, which was typical for me. I found a parking spot only half a block away from his house, a miracle in itself because finding parking in the Bronx can be a very difficult task. I threw my bag over my shoulder and walked toward his side door, through the small white gate that stands at the height of my hip. I walked over to the side window of the first floor. I knocked and the white shade shook from the vibrations of my knocking. I yelled, "It's me."

My yiayia, as she always did, greeted me warmly. She yelled to pappou, "Perry, your grandson is here." Then back to me, "He'll be right there, honey." I walked back through the gate to the front of the house. I waited a moment and the garage door slowly began to rise. I quickly ducked my head under the door, mostly because I am perpetually impatient, and there he was.

Pappou was wearing a white v-neck undershirt tucked into khakis, and *pandofles*, or sandals, and black socks. His hair was brushed back and his eyes were bright and alert. He hugged me and put one hand in the space where my jaw meets my neck and gave me a slight smack as a gesture of endearment.

I immediately prepared for the first of the three questions he always asked. "How are you, Perrymou?" With his hand still on my jaw, I said "I'm good, how's it going?" He smiled and said "Good, come see yiayia."

As I walked in, I was confronted with the second question, "How goes the school?" I turned back for a moment, "It's good ... I have to ask you something." He responded "Ok, Perrymou."

I saw yiayia and she raised her arms into the air, *zeibekiko*, Greek dancing style, to express that she was happy to see me. We embraced. Then as we broke our hug, pappou asked the third and final question as I was sitting down at the dining room table. "How goes the girl?" he asked with a smile.

"Still looking," I replied. He put his hand on my shoulder and said, "*Endaxi*," or "ok."

After yiayia asked if I was hungry, and then looked annoyed but still hospitable when I said no, I asked about the book. Pappou immediately understood what I was referring to although we hadn't spoken about it in a decade. It took him 15 minutes of rummaging through the closet next to his desk before he found it.

"Perry," he asked me, "why do you want me to find this book?"

I told him I was going to use it for my graduate school thesis.

"Graduate school thesis!" he appeared somewhat nervous. "You will make sure it's safe?"

"Of course, pappou."

Then he gave me a sly smile. "But Perry, you don't read Greek."

"I guess I'll find someone to translate it," I said.

"Ah, Nαι, yes, you will need someone to translate my brother's words."

"Exactly, pappou."

"And where will you find someone, Perry?" Again he gave me a wry smile, as he looked me in the eye. "How will someone know what my brother and I were thinking?"

I smiled and nodded in agreement with his argument.

"Well" he said as if the idea had just occurred to him, "I could translate."

I smiled back at him and only took a few seconds to realize that this would be our project, together. He put his hand on my shoulder and then stuck it out towards me. We shook hands.

With a grin, I said "Ok, let's go."

And so we agreed I would meet with him every week, and he would tell me all over again, the stories of the killing, of the blood, of the planting, of the children, of fathers and sons, mothers and daughters, of brothers killing brothers, of the harvest, of treachery, of bravery and salvation. I walked to my car after this first conversation fully aware that I made him a promise that was not to be broken.

When I returned a week later, we started with the ritual that would, more or less, begin each story. My pappou would sit in his chair in the living room, waiting. When I entered the room, he always stood up and walked towards me with open arms. He invariably said, "Ah, it's the writer." We would hug and kiss. He always asked me the same three questions and I would greet my yiayia as she was sitting on the couch. When we hugged and kissed, she would smile and ask me, as always, if I wanted to eat something. I usually said no. She would, as usual, be slightly annoyed, and I, of course, always told her that I had already eaten. She would put some kind of food on the table anyway which I would inevitably eat.

Then we three walked into the dining room and sat down at the dining room table that became our work desk. Pappou sat across from me. On our first day speaking about his story, he began by looking at me directly in a very formal way. He sat straight. His blue eyes were shinning. His gaze was clear and sharp. His full head of gray hair was flecked with some strands of white and was meticulously brushed back from his face. He dressed that day as he did for all of our meetings, in a variation of the same clothes—a button-down flannel shirt with sleeves rolled up, his shirttails tucked into a pair of crisp, pressed khakis.

This was how he dressed years earlier when he was working full time with my father in the laundromats. Now, our project was to be his new work, and as such, he dressed for the part. My grandfather had one set of clothes for relaxing in the house, one set for work, another for going out to eat or to go shopping, and then there was his most important look, his church clothes. The only carry over in attire were his church socks, which he often wore while sitting around the house, relaxing.

Yiayia enjoyed sitting with us. She would smile and nod and follow the conversation. She was also very helpful when my pappou had trouble translating certain Greek words, phrases, or expressions. She was born in America and her English vocabulary was much larger than my grandfather's. She would gently tap pappou on the arm when he was searching for a word, he would look at her, she would smile and nod toward me, perhaps supply a word or two. Then pappou would calm down and resume telling the story in English.

She also had a habitual way of dressing in a long black skirt worn by traditional older Greek women and a long-sleeved blouse, usually blue or white. Her hair was always nicely combed. They were the perfect portrait of an elderly Greek-American couple—attractive, proud and comfortable about who they were and what they had accomplished.

When we were settled in, my grandfather reached for his brother's notebook. He never opened it right away. Instead he placed one hand flat on the cover, the other on the table. Then he would lean forward and place both his elbows on the table and ask, "What do you want to know, Perrymou?"

I would answer: "What do you want to tell me?"

He always started by reading briefly, silently, to himself, from the old notebook to revive his memories, and then the story would begin.

***

The First Story:

Our homeland, Perrymou, Ελλάδα μας, Greece, is not just a land in tourist brochures where they show off our sunny islands, or ancient ruins, or modern busy cities like Athens, or those pretty little fishing villages with painted wooden boats and white stone houses that are built on steep hillsides over the water.

There is also the north of Greece, a beautiful land of tall mountains and deep green valleys. This place has clear blue lakes and small fast rivers. Everything is rich, fertile, and very green in the summertime, but it can also be cold and silent, and everything is covered in snow during our long winters.

These places change violently with the times. We Greeks from the mountains, we can be warm and sunny like the vineyards on a hot day, or cold and distant like ice in winter.

This is also the area that brought WWII to Greece. Our mountains and our village are near the Albanian border. They are in an area called Epirus, a territory that was fought over in modern days between Greece and Albania. After World War I, when Turkish control over that part of the world ended forever, πάλι καλά ("All is good"), North Epirus was given to Albania and South Epirus was given to Greece. This was not before the Turks killed hundreds of thousands of Greeks and Assyrians and over one million Armenians.

Then, Perry, in the 1930s, when I was just a little boy, there was a terrible depression. Everyone lost all their money. You must know about this from your studies, no? Well, the people were angry and dictators came to power. There was Franco in Spain, and a man named Salazar in Portugal. And that's when that bastard Hitler ruled Germany and that fool Mussolini ran Italy.

But, Perry, I have to say, we also had our own fascist dictator, a man named Ioannis Metaxas, who thought Mussolini was a great, great man. But, μερικές φορές ο διάβολος παίρνει λόγω του. (He spat the words. Yiayia tapped him on the arm. He frowned.) Oh yes, in English, yes, sometimes the devil gets his due.

On October 28, 1940, at 4:00 in the early morning, after an elegant party at the German embassy, the Italian Ambassador, a man named Emmanuel Grazzi, went to see Metaxas and said to Metaxas: Greece has to let Italian forces enter Greek territory or Greece and Italy will be at war.

When Metaxas heard what Grazzi had to say, he made maybe one of the only good decisions he ever made. He said, Οχι, No! and that, Perry, is why Greeks all over the world celebrate October 28, Επέτειος του Όχι, Oxi Day, as one of our important holidays.

In the summer of 1939, Italy had occupied Albania in order to create an Italian presence in the Balkans. The southernmost province of Albania, Albanian Epirus or North Epirus was a territory with historic links to Greek Epirus or South Epirus. In ancient times, all of Epirus and the nearby island of Corfu was a Greek province that was, briefly, the most important Greek state when Epirus controlled large portions of Southern Italy. The term "Pyrrhic victory," meaning, to win a battle but lose the war, comes from the Greek ruler Pyrrus who won victories against the Romans but eventually lost everything to the Roman Empire. Anyway, Perry, Epirus was Roman, then Byzantine, then Ottoman until after World War I, when it was split between Albania in the north and Greece in the south. But it remained mostly Greek, and the people spoke a dialect of Greek.

So, in November, after Metaxas said no to having Italian troops in Greece, Mussolini ordered the Italian army in Albania to invade Greece by marching from North Epirus in Albania into South Epirus in Greece. This was the beginning of World War II for Greece. After the Italians invaded, our country was very united and we fought heroically, especially in those mountains where I was living when I was a young boy. Our Greek soldiers were trained mountaineers, and the brave mountain women, the women of our village, my mother and her sisters, my aunts, all volunteered and carried food and ammunition through deep snow over high mountain passes to support our soldiers as they resisted the Italians.

By December of 1940, there was a great counteroffensive by our Greek army that not only retook South Epirus but they were also able to push back the Italians deep into Albania. At the end of that fighting, Greece controlled almost all of North Epirus where they set up defensive positions called the Metaxas Line. That was one of modern Greece's greatest victories, and it happened against huge odds. It was also the first Allied victory against the German/Italian alliance that was sweeping across Europe and North Africa with little resistance.

So those were the times and that was the land and those were the people who were your ancestors, Perrymou, and now I can tell you our family's story.

Our village, Λάγκα (Lagka) in the province of Kastoria was a very small village with maybe, oh…maybe 750 people. We had no running water in our houses. Instead, we had a fountain in the central village square where the women of Lagka would collect water and carry it in large jugs to our homes. There was no electricity. There were no electric lights. We used lanterns and torches to move around at night. There was only one telephone, and we never had any newspapers unless someone brought one from the city. We were not συνδεδεμένος (he looked toward yiayia who said, "Connected") naí, yes, connected to the outside world.

And, during winter, we were really cut off from the rest of Greece because Lagka was buried in snow. We survived on the food we put away during the spring, summer and early fall, and we all shared whatever we had with our neighbors.

Before the war started, no one in the other parts of Greece paid any attention to us. We had a mayor, one priest, and one head teacher. Each of these officials was respected and each of them earned our respect.

The mayor was a good man and a kind man who cared about everything in the village that needed to be dealt with, and he did that without ever getting any help from the central government. He did it all himself, and since he was not paid a salary, we all took care of him just as he took care of us.

The teacher was another important man. He ran our local school from his own home, and he wanted to make sure all of us had an education. It was a simple, one-room school on the first floor of his house—all the children, both boys and girls of different ages, studied together, and the older children helped teach the younger children. There were few textbooks and not a great deal of reading material, but everyone was expected to learn to read and write modern Greek, and to master addition, subtraction and basic mathematic equations. Our "science" came from the practical experience of planting crops, caring for the land, and hunting and raising animals. Our moral and spiritual training came from studying the Greek Orthodox religion and the glorious history of ancient Greece and our later struggles to become a free and independent nation again.

Our teacher donated a piece of his own precious land to the village school and we turned it into a garden. Children, from the very small ones to teenagers, came together to work on this garden, and it became something very, very beautiful. We planted all sorts of vegetables from tomatoes to peppers, and we carefully marked them so we knew what we planted as it grew. During the winter, all of the children brought wood to our teacher's home to keep all of us warm during our lessons.

Our priest was also very important. I remember that many, many times he would visit our home and ask my parents how we were doing in school. If any of us had problems, he would take the time to tutor us himself. If we were sick, he did what he could to find medicine. When the old people were dying, he helped care for them and comfort them and their families. Everyone in the village went to church every Sunday, and church service was an occasion that brought us all together in prayer no matter what problems we had.

In those days, we didn't have much, only what we needed. And we had each other. I was the second oldest of seven boys. There was Panayiotis—he wrote this notebook here—me, Pericles, Harileous, Demetrios, Efthemios, Euripides, and Philipas. My mother's name was Ourania and my father's name was Athanasios. Nine of us. That was our family.

My father was very thin but very strong; he had high cheekbones and a slightly pointed nose. He always wore a hat with a brim in the front. He dressed very nicely all the time, and he was a very neat man.

Father was a tailor, and a tailor was a craftsman. We needed a tailor in the village, because there were no stores carrying ready-made clothes, so everything was done by hand. Although factories in the cities manufactured the cloth, it was the tailors working in their workshops in the small villages that cut and sewed the final garments. My father made everything, from everyday clothes for men and women and children, to valuable items for wedding dowries, to rough blankets to keep everyone warm in the winter.

My mother was a short woman with thick, wavy black hair and round cheeks. She always wore a big smile and a dress. When she was not working in our house, she worked in the fields, farming. She was loving and kind, but she was also *shpirto*, that's a word from Albanian that we used for people with a fiery personality and sharp brains. When she thought no one was looking, she used to sneak cigarettes, but we all knew she did it.

I was closest with Panayiotis. We were always together. He stood a bit taller than me, and he had a lanky build. I was the shorter one, but I had wider shoulders. We both had coal black hair and dark, olive skin. We both had blue eyes. The other children in the village would make fun of our blue eyes, calling us cats. They would yell, "Γάτες!" ("Cats!"), when they saw us coming down the road. All our brothers had blue eyes, and when the children would mock us, we would end up fighting with them. Mostly it was Panayiotis and I who did the fighting. Then we would fight and wrestle with each other. When we went to school, we went together. We studied together. We did everything together.

Our home was very simple. It was built from wood and stone. On the first floor, we had a kitchen and a separate room for storing food. There was a small living room where we had a fire burning and where we would light candles so we could read and study. On the second floor, there was a bedroom for my parents and a bedroom for the seven boys.

There was another space at the back of the house where my father had his shop. He learned to be a tailor when he was fifteen, and he spent three years as an apprentice learning the trade. He was very good at his craft, and he made clothes for the entire village upon request, and he fitted them for each person. The house always smelled like leather.

The other houses in the village were more or less the same as our house, and most of the other men in the village, along with their wives and children, farmed the harsh, stony mountain land and developed other skills to provide some cash or items to barter for necessities. There were woodworkers, carpenters, and stonemasons, a shoemaker, a barber who, along with his wife, could tend to very simple medical and dental emergencies until the person could visit the doctors in Kastoria. There was a butcher although many butchered their own animals, and two small stores that stocked basic foodstuffs like sugar and salt and boxed or canned goods. There were two very simple *tavernas* where mostly men would gather to talk politics, discuss village affairs or conduct business. A blacksmith whose forge was used for all kinds of metalworking. In the winter, some villagers trapped rabbits, fox, ermine and mink, and then dried and scraped and stretched the pelts to be sent to the furriers in Kastoria where the skins were shaped and sewn into garments.

My father was not just a tailor. He was very skilled at many tasks where he used his hands. Panayiotis and I would go into the mountains with him and watch him split open trees to get pitch to burn. Then we would place the pitch in metal lanterns to give us light so we could stay up, sometimes until midnight, studying together. When our grandmother put us to sleep, she made sure that we said our prayers every night. We stood next to our beds, dropped to our knees, crossed ourselves, and said a prayer. Then we repeated this ritual ten times before we finally climbed into bed.

Both Panayiotis and I were very good at our studies. Before we were old enough to go to school, our parents taught us our letters and how to count, so we were prepared. We had a desire to learn. Both of our parents could read and write, which was unusual for our village. They appreciated learning because, when they were young, they were forced to sneak into school at night, since the Ottoman Turks, who ruled Greece, would not let them study in the Greek language.

Our life was simple. Each morning, when we woke up, we sat together and ate breakfast, mostly a piece of bread with butter. Then we would go off to school. My father went to his shop and my mother went to the fields. When we came home from school, we helped my mother in the fields.

My mother welcomed our help because she was working very hard through the morning and early afternoon. I remember her hands were rough from working, but her touch was always soft. She had a special ability to be both tough and gentle, and she raised us with this demanding love. When we were tired in the field, she didn't let us leave. Instead, she started singing. When she saw us get worried or tired she placed her hands on our shoulders and started singing the old Greek songs about love, exile, freedom, and pain. Ναι, yes, yes, I do remember she would look at us and start singing what I call her Wheat Songs.

After we worked in the field, it was time to go home, eat a simple meal—soup, maybe a bit of meat or cheese, and then study. Our mother always insisted that we study. All seven of us boys. She kept us in line. The whole village respected our family, and my mother was the center of our family.

We lived in poverty, but everyone did, so it was not special. The mountains of northern Greece had been a forgotten part of the Ottoman Empire for centuries. We were left alone and that was good because the only demands the Turks made upon us was that we pay our taxes to Istanbul, but being left alone also meant we received no money from the Ottomans, and because we were not connected to the modern world, our village life remained very simple. Then, when the kingdom of Greece gained its independence in 1832 with the

Treaty of Constantinople, we were still forgotten because the new government was controlled by the French, the Russians and the British who had defeated the Ottomans. They installed a German king, the Bavarian Prince Otto, because the Great Powers did not want a strong Greece independent of their influence. Besides, the new kingdom had a very small population, less than 800,000 people.

The Greeks fought a lot of wars over the next 100 years as they tried to unite all the Greek people in the Balkans and Asia Minor into one country. They gained more territory when they supported the Allies in World War II, and the population increased to over three million, but battles between the populist democrats who wanted to get rid of the king, and the royalists who wanted to keep a king created divisions that split the country to this day, Perry. So Greeks started fighting Greeks, and we mountain people remained poor no matter which side was in power.

The whole village worked the fields together. As children, we all went everywhere our parents went, and we helped with the harvest working alongside them. We harvested wheat, rye, corn, beans, and lentils, and we worked in teams. In the spring we cleared the land of weeds and wild grass. We planted new crops. Then we carefully kept the fields clear of weeds so the wheat could grow clean and strong. Everything was done properly with attention to detail because every plant was valuable. We couldn't get tired. When we did harvest, we kept what we needed and took the rest to nearby cities to sell in the markets.

The men made the day trips to the cities, exchanged their goods, and came home. We were excited when we waited for our father to return late at night after he left so early in the morning. We waited to get our small gifts that our father purchased from the market—mostly some kind of candy. One simple piece of candy for each of us brought such joy! My father walked up to the front door and we were all waiting for him in a clump of pushing and shoving children. He put one piece of candy into each of our hands and we devoured it. When the weather was warm, all us brothers would greet our father and then stay outside playing.

Each season was special in Lagka. Even the winter, although it made everything very difficult, was a beautiful picture. The summer and spring were especially beautiful. In April, when the snow melted, when spring came, everything turned green with new life and the wild flowers bloomed on the hillsides. There were green trees everywhere all the way into the far distance until our eyes saw the cool blue waters of the lake. It was a beautiful life, but it changed a lot when I was still just a boy.

After Mussolini ordered the invasion of Greece, and the Italian soldiers pushed their way south through Epirus, our beautiful mountains were filled with the thunder of bombs, raging fires spread by the fighting, and clouds of thick white ash that rained down on everything. Then, when we fought back and defeated the Italians, it was peaceful again in the spring of 1941, but Hitler, furious with Mussolini for the Italian humiliation at the hands of the Greeks, flooded German troops and tanks from Bulgaria into Thessaloniki in northeastern Greece. The German panzer advance was relentless, and despite valiant Greek resistance, Greece was forced to surrender. Then the Italians came back into Greece from Albania and occupied our mountains along with the Germans. Our poor country was swallowed by the beast.

But even before the worst horrors of the occupation destroyed our little village, I experienced the terror of what was coming. A Thessaloniki Jew named Marko Yehoshua was the regional sales manager for Singer sewing machines. Before the war, the Jews of Thessaloniki, a city they called Salonika, were the majority population there. They were originally Jews from Spain who were thrown out of that country a long time ago by the Spanish queen, Isabella, who in that same year, 1492, sent Christopher Columbus to America. They spoke Ladino, Spanish really, among themselves, not the Yiddish you hear German and Eastern European Jews speak. But they also spoke Greek and considered themselves Greeks. They were very powerful in Greek political and commercial life, and they were very passionate soldiers in the Greek army, fighting against the Italians and especially against the Germans.

I had seen Marko many times when he visited Lagka to sell equipment to my father. He was a kind and gentle man who often visited our house just to chat even if there was no sale to be made, because he and my father were friends. Somehow he sent word to us that he had been trapped in Argos, a city on the Peloponnese, the southern part of Greece, by the rapid German advance and occupation of that peninsula. He was desperate to get back to Northern Greece where there were many Greek Jews from Thessaloniki fighting against the occupation. Marko told my father he had a contact that could smuggle him out of the country to Palestine if he could get to the mountains in the north.

My father sent me to Argos because he thought the Germans wouldn't stop and question a young boy who wasn't old enough to be in the army. He was right, and I was able to get to Argos without being stopped at any of the German roadblocks. I found Marko hiding in the factory of one of his Greek clients, a man who was willing to protect him until I got there.

Our plan was to travel together and I was to be his son. I brought a fake identity card for him, and we found old clothes that, when he dressed in them, made him look like he lived in a Greek village. I remember being worried about his hands because they were soft, not calloused, not the kind of hands I saw every day, not the hands of a person who worked in the field, so we made him wear gloves.

When we left Argos, there were many Greeks walking along the roads and hitching rides. Total chaos was happening all across Greece, and people did their best to avoid being caught up in the fighting. I was used to all this confusion because I saw so many crazy things when I travelled down to Argos. But Marko was very nervous. Although he was the adult and I was the child, I worried about him and I tried to tell him jokes to calm him down.

Our return to the north was working very well until we got to the bridge that crossed over the Megdovas River near the village of Episkopi. The Germans were very alert around our bridges because they were prized targets.

There was a huge, long line of people carrying all their things trying to cross the bridge, and we grew very nervous as we slowly came up to the checkpoint. Suddenly, not far ahead in line, a woman started crying when two German soldiers dragged a young man out of the line. She wrapped her arms tightly around the man, and so the soldiers also dragged the woman, who was kicking and screaming, out of the line. Then, at the edge of the bridge, one of the soldiers pulled out his pistol from his holster and shot both the man and the woman in the back of the head. Blood spurted from their skulls as they collapsed onto the ground. Then the shooter yelled to another soldier and the two of them lifted the bodies and heaved them over the bridge into the muddy waters of the Megdovas.

After that, Marko was shaking so badly he couldn't stop, and I was terrified. But so was everyone around us. As it turned out, this was a good thing. We were no more upset than the others being questioned, and the German soldiers didn't want any more problems, so they only asked simple questions, made quick investigations of our ID cards, and hurried everyone on through the checkpoint.

We did make it back to Kastoria. A few days later, we brought Marko to the Albanian border where we spoke to villagers there who would hide him until he could escape to Palestine. The villagers there were very friendly and they, like many Albanians at that time, took care of Jews. They had besa—they will die before they go against their word. These were noble people, our neighbors in Albania.

After we left him, I never saw Marko again. I don't know if he made it to Palestine. I hope so, because in 1944, the Ladino Jews of Salonika were rounded up and transported in cattle cars by train to Auschwitz where they were murdered. Almost no Greek Jews survived the war. I had already seen that beast face-to-face on my journey with Marko, and I knew that the beast killed.

As the fighting against the Italians grew stronger in the mountains, we worried how we could save our big family with its nine members. The fierce battles were destroying our land. Fires burned off the grain in the fields. To make money, we cut down trees and crafted spoons and other things including tools for digging and trenching. We made wooden packsaddles and many other items that would be useful for carrying food and ammunition on mountain trails. We also made charcoal for heating and cooking.

Then we melted down our metal objects on the blacksmith's forge, and we made braziers to hold burning charcoal. We shaped iron that could be used for grills and roasting spits. We carried all of these things on our backs to the city, and the long walk seemed to last forever when we carried those heavy things down the mountainside. But we had no choice: if we did not go and trade what we could for wheat and corn and then return to our younger brothers and our mother, they would not have survived, so we walked.

Still, there was not enough to eat, so Panayiotis and I found a job at a restaurant in Kastoria. Since we often worked late into the night, we made beds out of the chairs in the restaurant and we slept there only to start work again at daybreak. That restaurant was able to stay in business because we served the soldiers who were fighting the Italians. When the soldiers left after eating, Panayiotis and I swept up their leftovers and that was what we ate. That was how hard those times were. If we could save food for our family by eating crumbs, we did.

But the restaurant couldn't stay open after our Greek soldiers were defeated. We were forced to leave Kastoria and go back home.

When we returned home the second time, the situation was very, very bad. The fields were completely empty. Our father couldn't make any money in his shop. No one in the village had money for clothes; they didn't even have money for food. Mussolini's men, under Hitler's orders, began to take and kill our animals. This was the beginning of our starvation, just one of the many terrible things the beast forced upon us.

***

With that ominous closing phrase, my pappou set aside the plain white paper napkin he had been methodically folding and unfolding. Then he made a circle on the tabletop with his hands.

His hands were always a marvel to me. As a child and even in my adolescence, I would watch his hands very closely when he spoke to me. They were working hands. His skin had been bruised and torn, his fingers gnarled, his knuckles thick from years of manual labor—working on the farm in the mountains as a child, then as a dishwasher when he first came to America, and eventually as his own mechanic for the small chain of laundromats he owned. His hands were dark, sunbaked, olive on the outside, but perhaps only in contrast, very pale white on the inside. He often flung them around as he spoke. His hands were like his personality, both soft and hard.

In his appearance, pappou exhibited classical Stoicism. He walked with an erect posture, his chest out and chin up with an uncanny alertness for someone his age. His steps were very deliberate and confident, even when he slowed with advancing years. Life and business had hardened his exterior and made him tough, taciturn in speech and hot tempered when working.

These traits were juxtaposed to how he interacted with his family, his neighbors and his friends. His story about Marko reminded me about the close relationship he had with his Albanian neighbors in the Bronx. When they first arrived on the block, my pappou offered money to the father to help them get established. It was not a great amount, but it was from the love and respect pappou had for their culture. I have wondered if the story about Marko prompted this kindness toward a stranger.

As I was taking notes, my pappou leaned back in his seat. He locked his fingers and placed his hands between his chest and his stomach, and took a deep breath. He exhaled and thought to himself, and then he said, "You know, Perry, we didn't feel poor. We didn't have much, but that didn't mean anything because no one had much. No one had more than anyone else."

"That was why, when the war came, when starvation and death came to our village, our loss was more..." he searched for the right word, "σφοδρός..."

Yiayia said, "Intense."

"Ναί, yes, yes, intense. We began to *feel* poor. But when I say we felt like we were poor, I mean we felt like we lost something we once had. We felt 'lessness.' Is 'lessness' a word, Perry?"

Yiayia shook her head, no, but I shrugged. "Works for me."

"Before the war, we didn't feel the loss of 'anything more.' There *was* nothing more."

Yiayia nodded. "People had to work very hard, but I think they were happy."

"Yes," continued pappou, "work is not a bad thing. Your father and I, we work all the time. You've seen us. You've worked with us. And I see you. You also work all the time. You know work is..." he slapped the table, "...work is good." As his voice grew louder, yiayia laughed as she watched pappou's growing strength.

He continued: "Being tired isn't painful, it's a gift."

I laughed because I knew he was serious.

"Perry. I am an old man, yes, but I really find making things, growing tomatoes in my garden or taking care of yiayia, making her life better, those are the things that give me a happy heart." He touched his hand to this chest.

Yiayia smiled. Pappou placed his hand atop hers. "Yes, working is a good thing."

This mentality was one that I was very familiar with. Both my father's side of the family and my mother's side, which was in construction, understood the value and privilege of good, honest, hard, work. Everyone in the family, more or less, was an entrepreneur or a teacher or both. The environment I grew up in, and still live in, is one in which work is often the centerpiece of conversation.

My pappou sighed and slumped back into his chair. "You asked me about φιλότιμο (*philotimo*) a long time ago, when you were a little boy, the first time I told you stories from Panayiotis's notebook. Do you remember?"

I nodded.

"*Philotimo* is one of the most important words in the Greek language because it describes… ah, it's so hard to translate or even explain."

Yiayia added, "Maybe honor, loyalty to family… to…" She also struggled to find the right words.

I gazed at them patiently as they tried to define the word.

"*Philotimo* is a…" pappou waved a hand in the air. "It's a Greek thing, Perrymou, self-respect, ah, doing good, like it tells me what kind of person you are, how you were raised, things like that."

Yiayia interrupted again, "*Philotimo* is a virtue, a spiritual feeling."

I grew up in the Greek Orthodox church with all of its incredibly powerful symbols and rituals—the mosaic icons, the gold braided vestments on the gray bearded priests, the pungent incense, the smoking beeswax candles and the Byzantine chanting that often lifted me from day-to-day reality onto a plane of consciousness that I never fully understood as a child.

"A spiritual feeling… like in church?" I asked.

Pappou paused and fiddled with his napkin again. Yiayia smoothed the pleats on her skirt, her thin, slightly curved fingers moved slowly back and forth across the black polyester, a movement that in the silence made a soft hissing sound.

"Yes and no," said yiayia.

Pappou continued: "When we walked down that mountain loaded up with more than we could carry. When we slept on chairs. When we ate crumbs from the soldiers' meals. When we returned to Lagka where there was nothing, nothing, and they took us in. That was *philotimo*—a sense that we owed everything to each other, to our families and our village, and we should do whatever we could to honor our debt to each other."

I responded to this explanation with a smile and a nod. As a philosophy student, I of course enjoyed hearing this explanation of *philotimo*. I knew pappou believed in what he was saying, and I knew that was how he viewed the world. This was to be taken seriously.

"I like that. That's important then."

I wrote down the word and circled it.

He continued. "Life can be very hard, Perrymou," he said with a slight hitch in his voice as he glanced at my yiayia, "but *philotimo* gives strength and meaning in the bad times." He stared directly into my eyes and added somewhat fiercely, "*Philotimo* gives us a reason to walk through hell for one another. *Philotimo* is everything."

"Everything?"

"Honoring our blood. Our family. Life itself."

Then, suddenly, his eyes lost some of their intensity. His shoulders slumped. His neck bent forward and his head tilted toward me. "Ah, Perrymou, Είμαι κουρασμένος ("I am tired"). Enough for today?"

"Sure, pappou."

"You know the way out, Perry."

"Yes, yes of course."

"I think yiayia and I will just sit for awhile."

I stood and looked at the two of them. He was still holding her hand. I asked, "Can I get you anything?"

He shook his head, no. Yiayia smiled at me and also shook her head.

I left them there holding hands with each other and walked out the front door into a warm Bronx afternoon. I was convinced that we had started something meaningful. I knew after our conversation that I had a debt to pappou and my yiayia, and now that we had started the stories, I would finish the task we were undertaking.

A slight breeze was blowing. The street didn't look like a Greek street would look. It didn't smell like the Greek mountains would smell. But I was filled with Greece as I walked toward my car.

I sat in my car for a moment and felt a smile come across my face. I realized that I now had a new mission, a new aim, and a new duty to fulfill with this work. I knew I had just received a new blessing and a new obligation.

CHAPTER 2

We're Not Made of Ashes

"...what can be more ridiculous than for them to utter the names of family ties with the lips only, and not to act in the spirit of them?"
—**Plato, Republic,** *Book V.*

I grew up in the Pelham Parkway section of the Bronx, in a semi-attached brick house with three floors. My family lived in the top two and at one time other family members lived on the bottom floor.

Pelham Parkway is not so far away from Manhattan, but those relatively short distances can mean a huge difference in neighborhoods. We lived near the eastern edge of the Bronx Zoo, near Pelham Bay.

Our house on Seymour Avenue was a few blocks from where my pappou lived on Mickle Avenue. Our church, Zoodohos Peghe, on Bruckner Boulevard, was only a short distance further east just across from the heavy traffic of the Bruckner Expressway and the thick-limbed old trees and green lawns of Pelham Bay Park. The church is also right across from Willow Lane where my Italian mother grew up. My mother and father met in Pelham Bay Park, and they began a Greek-Italian romance that's continued for over thirty years.

During the summer, my sister, Christina, and I would spend days on end at our grandparents' houses, switching between the two families depending on the day. It was a genuinely cross-cultural experience. My mother was working as an adjunct professor and going to school for her doctorate during our early childhood. Since she started work a couple of weeks before we were back at school, she shuttled us to our grandparents' houses during the day and then picked us up after dinner.

When I was playing at my pappou's house, I really felt Greek. There was a decorative shield, depicting Achilles dragging Hector's body around the gates of Troy hanging next to their television in the kitchen. I was forever distracted from trying to watch a Yankee's baseball game by Achilles gazing at me with an aggressive, triumphant look on his face. I was pretty certain that none of my friends at school had mythological figures staring at them when they ate pizza.

The American foods often included grilled cheese, Coca-Cola, and Häagen-Dazs, which is from the Bronx, by the way. Those would be accompanied by the perpetual presence of grapes, many of which pappou picked himself since he had grape vines in his yard for years, homemade baklava, and pita. They would both cook, and took a great deal of pride in having us over as kids and, of course, feeding us constantly.

My pappou came to America with close to nothing except a suit made by his father and the equivalent of $37.00. When he met my yiayia, she was pretty Mollie Nicholas, a Greek-American girl born and raised in the Chelsea neighborhood of Manhattan. That area is now a completely gentrified, artsy and genteel neighborhood, but in those days it was a mixture of industrial and commercial, high-rise apartments and tenements. He was Pericles, the young immigrant who was working as a dishwasher and living with six other men in a one-room apartment.

Pericles and Mollie hit it off immediately and began dating the day after they were introduced. When he started earning decent money, pappou said to Mollie, "All I can give you are my hands and my heart." She said that was more than enough.

After their wedding, they moved into an apartment on Post Avenue in Inwood on the far northern tip of Manhattan.

My father was not their first-born. Yiayia's first child was also a boy. They named him Athanasios, after his grandfather. But after giving birth, my yiayia's life-long dream to have a son was snatched away because Athanasios was born with a severe case of jaundice, and he died a few weeks later.

Despite their deep sorrow, pappou and yiayia tried to have another child, and the second time the baby was healthy. They named her Barbara, after St. Barbara—the church that welcomed pappou when he first came to America. Three years later, my father, Vasilis, or Bill, was born.

In my Italian grandparents' house, I felt really Italian because I spent most of my time there with my grandfather, Giuseppe, who was blind and was born in Italy, and my grandmother, Elizabeth who was born in America but is also Italian. My grandmother would make macaroni and meatballs on a daily basis as the radio in the kitchen often played Dean Martin, Frank Sinatra and Pavarotti, among other Italian and Italian-American artists.

I am named after my Italian grandfather with my middle name. He went blind when he was 50, but he was an unbelievably energetic man. He ran our family construction business and was brilliant and passionate about what he did. Although he was walking through a horrible nightmare every day once he went blind, he never complained or let on that it was difficult. Looking back I believe going blind must have initially felt like a death sentence because of his boundless energy.

I remember my mother would tell him, "Dad, watch after Perry." She would then whisper to me "Perry, watch after grandpa."

We were inseparable. Even though Giuseppe was blind he would always plan things for us to do together. We seldom sat still. We played dominos, cards (I never lied to him about what cards were showing on the table), arm wrestled, and went for walks. We spent hours walking around the Pelham Bay section of the Bronx just talking and stopping here and there for food, a drink, or to sit at the park. We both moved constantly.

When I arrived early in the morning, I would get to see what I now understand as one of his most important and philosophical rituals. Every morning my grandmother, Elizabeth would ask "You want to do the stairs?" He would always respond "Yea, give me a minute."

He would stand up from the couch and walk past the dining room, past the kitchen and into their bedroom. After getting dressed, he would leave the bedroom, walk past the kitchen and make a slight left to reach the back door. He always smiled and waved toward the living room and I would follow him.

A broom leaned against the wall on the right side of the door, just where it always was in the morning. He would open the door and grab the broom. Then he would step through the open door and run his other hand along the wall as we walked down the stairs to the outside landing of the house. The stairs went to the landing followed by seven steps that led to the sidewalk.

When we made it outside, my grandfather would always greet the world with a smile. Then he would begin sweeping the stairs. Each stair got three good sweeps, and he would go up and down a few times. I would sit at the top of the stairs and watch, as he would often make conversation as he swept.

There was one day in particular that I always hold in my memory and return to from time to time. It was like any other day, except it rained. He looked up at me and said, "Is it getting cloudy?"

"Yea," I replied. "I think it might rain."

"I only need a minute."

"You'll be okay."

He gave the final step a few more sweeps and then said "How'd I do?"

I replied, "Good work."

"Alright, let's go inside."

We went back inside and it started raining. The drops pounded the windows as we sat in the living room. He turned to me with a smile and said, "Good thing we got the stairs done."

I smiled and said, "Yea, we got it done."

Going blind in the middle of one's life would be a tremendous burden for anyone, and my grandfather's boundless energy was restrained by his condition. Still, he smiled as he swept those stairs, laughed as we sat and talked, passionately compete while we played dominos with lifted dots so he could feel them with his fingers.

As a young child, I often thought of the practical questions associated with his blindness as he swept the stairs. How does he know when to stop? How does he know if they're dirty or not? I never said anything; it would have been rude. I understood that he was doing the work because my grandmother asked him to and ultimately because he chose to. He would always smile, always, but especially when he was tasked with something like sweeping the stairs.

I now understand my grandfather with much greater clarity. He was struck by the absurd and random powers of chance—his sight was taken. Yet while he swept, he bravely bore his burden with courage and the awareness of his power to choose how he dealt with his fate.

My grandfather was initially confronted with a profound sense of powerlessness and detachment from day-to-day reality that was undoubtedly jarring. These are the same feelings that often accompany our initial response to the absurd torrent of chance. Misfortune strikes, and we see ourselves losing control and attacked. But in fact, we are never out of control of our ability to choose how we react to misfortune. That's what my Italian grandfather taught me.

He went from being a sighted man to a completely blind man over the span of a few months. His vision slowly closed until there was only darkness. But what occurred in the following moment was a true triumph. He chose not to define the rest of his life with this disability. He chose to remain the man he had always been.

Just as each day he would grow older, the radio would play different songs, food would taste slightly different, or I would have different stories to share with him and he with me, he understood that his blindness was just another change. He understood that it was up to him, and only him, to bear this burden and move forward through the darkness. He chose to do so and in so doing, he became his own light and the creator of his new life.

I remember I smiled at his playful comment about the rain—that it was a "Good thing we got the stairs done," as I often smiled in his presence, even though I knew that he could not see me. Nonetheless, my smiles were genuine and were a result of my choosing to be happy and of my choice to understand that even though he could not see my smile, he knew that we were happy in that moment.

Giuseppe passed away when I was a sophomore in high school, long before I could even begin to articulate all that he taught me, but when he was alive, my Italian grandfather and my pappou were always best friends. They would call each other every day and see each other frequently. On those occasions when the extended family gathered together, Giuseppe sat at one head of our table and pappou sat at the other end.

I have often joked that I didn't see my father until I was about ten years old. He worked what seemed like 24/7 at the family laundromats and the two pizzerias that my dad owned and operated on Broadway and Dyckman street in Inwood. I remember those stores vividly, because I often went along with my father and grandfather at 4:30 in the morning to open the stores. This was the beginning of my familiarity with getting up before the sun rises. It is a habit I would often return to through college and graduate school.

The day began with my father nudging my shoulder on a Saturday morning. My father and I first stopped at Twin Donut, where I always ordered a grilled cheese and milk. Cholesterol was not a concern. Then we climbed back into my father's old car that had neither air conditioning nor a functional heater, so we boiled in the summer and froze in the winter. That old green Buick Lesabre saw a lot of miles driving up and down Pelham Parkway and Inwood.

We would often meet pappou at the gate of the first laundromat we opened. One day, during winter, I made the mistake of saying that I was cold. We were standing outside shivering in the dark and had to use a blowtorch to unlock the frozen gate. My pappou turned to me and said, "Είσαι από τις στάχτες?" I had no idea what that meant. I squinted my eyes and looked up at my father, who was smiling down at me.

"He wants to know if you're made of ashes."

Still only half understanding, I stuck my chest out and said, "No!" Even as a nine-year-old I knew I should never show weakness in front of pappou. He placed his hand on my forehead and said, "Okay, Perrymou, help me lift the gate."

Pappou believed in toughness and he seized every opportunity to make me tough as well. He was absolutely fearless. He had a saying, *proto theos*, God willing, and he knelt when he prayed and feared God, but that was about it in terms of being afraid.

Thou shall not steal, especially not from us, became a very real motto of how we operated those stores. One day we were working on a washing machine by the front of the store, and we were not really paying attention to the rest of the store. As I was passing a tool to my father, I saw pappou looking toward the back. He tapped me on the shoulder and pointed to a teenager trying to steal quarters out of a machine. At the time we had been experiencing a rash of break-ins from local teenagers. They would try to break into the money boxes during the day, or go behind the machines and try to take loose quarters and run out down the street.

We both watched for a few more seconds as the teenager was grabbing quarters from behind a machine. Pappou turned toward a broomstick leaning on the wall. He snapped the bristled bottom off with is foot, handed me the stick and said "Don't let him steal from us." I hesitated for a moment and looked up at my father. My Dad looked at me, raised his eyebrows slightly, and nodded. I grabbed the stick, walked to the machine, started swinging and the kid ran out. I walked back to my father and pappou with a handful of quarters. Pappou looked at the quarters, patted me on the head and said, "*Endaxi*," or "okay," and then he asked that I get some tape so he could put the broomstick back together. I walked over to the toolbox and got the tape, sat down and started repairing the broomstick.

Pappou often reverted to Greek when he wanted to make a point. When we began to meet regularly and he was telling me his stories based on Panayiotis's journal, he would begin speaking Greek, and I would be glassy-eyed, totally lost, and unable to understand. During those moments, it was always yiayia who would notice my confusion.

I was prepared for more Greek when, in October, a month after our first meeting, our second meeting began. Pappou and yiayia were sitting in the living room when I entered. Pappou stood and greeted me. Yiayia asked me what I wanted to eat, and after I again declined her offer, we three headed for our "office" in the dining room. This time, as we sat down, pappou picked up a rubber band that had been lying on the table and began stretching it back and forth around his fingers and between his hands before he opened the book. I waited for him to begin, but he appeared nervous, hesitant. I asked him if anything was wrong.

He shook his head, no, but he still didn't begin.

I decided to get things rolling by telling him a memory I'd been thinking about, when he and my father and I were strolling down Dyckman Street at first light—dawn on a warm summer day—when the street cleaners were driving by, their giant brushes washing the street, and the garbage collectors were clattering the old metal garbage cans on the sidewalk, and he and my father had pockets bulging with coins from the laundromats, and I was so proud to be walking to work with my father and my pappou.

Suddenly pappou interrupted me, set aside the rubber band, laid both hands flat on the table, looked me straight in the eye, and said, "We don't have time to waste, Perrymou."

Then he opened the book.

***

The Second Story:

The mayor of Lagka, during those first days of the beast, was my uncle, Nicholas Rizopoulos. He was a good man who, after the occupation, became a priest. He looked like the rest of our family—his blue eyes shot out from his dark skin and his thick black hair.

One morning, Italian soldiers marched into our village and ordered my uncle to ring the bell in the central square. When the bell rang, we all had to leave our houses and go to the square. Everyone had to come out to the square, or there would be big trouble.

After taking all our food and all our animals they could find, the soldiers demanded we give them our guns.

My uncle said, "We have no guns."

So the soldiers selected men and women from the crowd and began to punch and kick them and beat them with their rifles. One of the Greek snitches, a traitor named Tasos, suddenly attacked my uncle, punching him in the face while my uncle had his arms held behind his back by soldiers. Tasos screamed at my uncle, "Where are the guns? I know you have hidden guns!"

My uncle again said, "We don't have guns."

The snitch had my uncle handcuffed, and told him, "Go to hell. You are going to the camps."

I started yelling from the crowd, but my voice was covered over by the grumbling from the people all around me. I tried to run toward my uncle when I saw him being dragged away by the soldiers, but the other villagers held me back.

Then, when the soldiers approached the edge of town, three old men stopped them. They spoke to the soldiers for a few minutes, and Tasos, that pig, ran over to the group to try and convince the soldiers to take my uncle away. All the πληροφοριοδότες [this word brought a nudge from yiayia], the informants, did this kind of thing, but after those few minutes, for whatever reason, the soldiers let my uncle go. He walked back into the square and I felt better.

After that incident with my uncle, things got worse. The Italians recruited more snitches and spies who came with the soldiers into all the villages, and they began killing everything. Mussolini's firing squads, led by these damned traitors, collected all the animals, the sheep, goats, lambs, cattle, horses, pigs, everything, and shot them. They had orders to leave nothing behind, not a single loaf of bread, not a single leaf on the trees. They killed people, too, and they gathered hostages and sent them to the camps in Thessaloniki.

They took groups of older people and locked them up in school basements. These basements became torture rooms where they brutally beat people until they passed out or worse. They grabbed people at random and took them into the town square and beat them with *phalange*—sturdy wooden poles. They bound their feet and hands and beat the soles of their feet. Whenever the children left school, the soldiers fired their guns into the sky to frighten them. Every day, people were detained and sent to camps. Everyone knew what was in store for those who were taken. They were given to the Germans and burned in the crematoriums, the death factories.

Once the soldiers had stolen everything from us and were demanding more, people were fed up with this treatment. Then the adults in the village began to organize and started preparing to revolt. For weeks they were getting ready so they could decide where the uprising would start, who would be involved, and when it would begin; everyone was buzzing with anticipation.

In the central mountains to the south of us, the anti-royalist, leftist partisans were dominated by the Greek communist party faction, the KKE. In February 1942, they created the Greek Peoples Liberation Army called ELAS (Ελληνικός Λαϊκός Απελευθερωτικός Στρατός), and many democratic and even non-political Greeks joined ELAS because they had become the largest and most effective partisan force. Their leader was a man named Athanasios Klaras, a soldier who fought in the Albanian wars and took the name Aris Velouchiotis (because Ares was the Greek god of war, and Velouchi was a famous Greek mountain). Velouchiotis organized his partisan groups to fight in the mountains because he knew the men were experienced mountain fighters who could easily outmaneuver the Italians and the Germans.

Meanwhile, the British secret service, afraid they were losing control of the Greek resistance, organized another group of partisan fighters who were more right-wing and loyal to the Greek king. They were called EDES, or the National Republican Greek League. Under pressure from the British who were supplying arms and intelligence to the partisans, ELAS and EDES worked together to plan and carry out the spectacular bombing of the bridge at *Gorgopotamos* that let the world know Greeks would never accept occupation by the Italians and the Germans.

But sadly, after that big success, the two partisan groups started fighting against each other for dominance within the Greek resistance movement. This fighting was a terrible tragedy that would one day, after World War II ended, develop into the horrible and disastrous Greek Civil War.

In our village, the revolt officially started when the men went into the mountains near the Albanian border and dug up the guns they had hidden there to make sure the weapons were not discovered by the Germans or the Italians. So, yes, Perry, there were guns after all. Then they brought all their weapons back down to Lagka. Everyone took part. All of the villagers, young and old, all the farmers, and the teacher, and the baker, and the shoemaker, and the tailor—my father,—and the mayor, the priest, and the women took part. We all gathered in the village square and lined up in rows of three. Everyone was angry and everyone wanted to play a part.

That was our moment to join the revolution! Suspense filled the air while we waited for the match to light an explosion. It was 5:00 PM when one of the members of the organizing committee, George Giannoulis, an accountant, appeared in front of the crowd. He stood proudly in a homemade army uniform with his chest sticking out. His mustache shook with excitement as he prepared to speak. Then he delivered an outburst against the occupiers. A flag fluttered behind him waving blue and white in the face of the grey sky. The entire village filled the air with sounds of excitement and hope. Another flag flew that read, ELAS. One of the villagers pointed out that the spelling was incorrect, that it had to be "ELLAS" to spell out "Greece." Giannoulis responded to the man by saying, "For me, this is correct. It does not spell Greece. It spells our fighting group." And so we became part of ELAS, The Greek People's Liberation Army.

The days and the weeks that followed the beginning of our revolt against the occupiers were days and weeks when we were covered in dust from the bombings by German and Italian warplanes. The airplanes hammered Nestorio, a village near ours, and then our village, Lagka. We were bombed every day. It rained death for weeks. Then, on March 25th at 3:30 PM, three large bombs were dropped on our village. They targeted our school, which was near my house, and one of the bombs destroyed our home. It turned the whole house into rubble.

We weren't in the house when the bomb fell, because we spent most of the time during the bombings hiding on a small mountain outside of our village. The mountain had rocks that formed caves where we hid when the airplanes came. We watched from one of those caves when the bombs fell.

After our village had been directly hit, the revolt got stronger, and everyone wanted revenge. Many people came from Nestorio and assembled in

Lagka. Men, women, and children all came to what was left of our village and it became the local headquarters for the Greek warriors. All our supplies were stored in the ruins. Our village became an armory, our gardens became ash, and all the people of Lagka became warriors. More and more people from the area arrived in our village to enlist with the rebels who we started calling αντάρτες, *andartes*, "guerillas." Everyone was awake and ready as the countdown began for the occupiers to attack us.

It wasn't long before Mussolini's soldiers brought reinforcements to fight. They hit us with tanks, motorized equipment, and aircraft. Their army was huge and their attacks were massive and relentless, but even so, they had little success because our people knew how to fight in the mountains. The more we were bombed, the more the people fought. Before long, everyone in our region near Kastoria had joined the uprising. Except for the snitches and the spies. But we didn't consider them to be Greeks. Tasos, that bastard, was paid back with the same coin he spent against us, and he was one of the first people who were executed by ELAS in our town. He was taken to the Kepseli Mountains and killed.

As our strength grew, British commandos were parachuted in by night, but Mussolini's planes still bombed Lagka daily. By the late fall of 1942, the entire village was empty. We lived in the caves we had dug into the mountainsides, and used the forest for cover from the bombs. We started creating even more caves and we reinforced them with lumber and earth. First, we built our caves in a dry spot to avoid the humidity. Second, we built them in a place where we could hide from the planes. We had to build them under trees or make our own camouflage so the planes couldn't see us. Still, the planes flew over the caves and dropped bombs at random. Sometimes, by chance, they hit us anyway.

We also made forest huts by following certain techniques. We cut round, but not very thick branches, three and a half to four meters in length, into the shape of a Greek "L" (Λ). Then we put each branch on top of the others to make the skeleton. Over the skeleton, we put taller logs and branches, and then squares of sod, soil with grass, to cover the skeleton. These took a lot of work to fit together so that the water from the rain did not fall into the pyramids. When it snowed, a blanket of snow covered the hut.

On one side we made a fireplace with a vent that removed the smoke very well. On another side we made a window for light. Finally, we made rough beds, so we didn't have to sleep on the ground. We collected all of our possessions such as clothes, blankets, and whatever else we had and kept them inside the huts or in the caves.

We lived with nothing; our houses had all been burned along with all of our belongings. Some of us had no shoes and others didn't even have a change of clothes. We planted rye on the slopes because we couldn't grow wheat on a mountainside. We planted potatoes and turnips and beets that could grow in mountain soil. We lived off of what grain we could recover from our fields and what we could find in the forest: wild plants, small animals, roots and berries. We did a thousand things to survive. Whenever we walked out from the forest, we saw that everything was destroyed. Whatever the bombs didn't destroy, the occupiers burned by hand.

It was a terrible time. Just terrible.

* * *

With that final statement, pappou closed the book. When he stopped talking, there were tears in yiayia's eyes. Throughout this story, as pappou told of the destruction of Lagka, each of his comments was echoed by yiayia's exclamations of shock and dismay at the conditions he described. Then she would add a nod of disapproval and the occasional gasp. But now she was quiet.

In the silence, pappou absentmindedly picked up the rubber band and again began stretching it through his fingers. I couldn't speak while the sheer brutality of what he had lived through sunk into my consciousness. I think, for the first time, I began to get a taste of how truly awful those events were, but pappou had spoken in such a calm voice that the terrors seemed unreal. He described the scenes with a clear sense of involvement and a vivid memory of the despicable events, but he was simultaneously so very matter-of-fact about his experiences.

My pappou reacted to all the hardships in his life with a similar attitude. He was able to express complete love, one might even say, unconditional love, alongside utter practicality and unquestioned faith. From everything I knew about him ever since he came to America, from everything I had experienced when I was with him, he did what he believed he had to do to the best of his ability for those he loved. And he appeared to face any and all hardships with equanimity.

It remained very quiet in the dining room except for my yiayia's occasional sniffles and the muffled sounds of cars and trucks passing by outside their window. Then pappou stood up, gathered a dish and a glass he had been using while he talked and went into the kitchen. Yiayia followed him. I heard him put his dishes in the sink. As I was putting my notes away, I noticed yiayia had left her glass on the table. I picked it up and brought it into the kitchen.

I said: "Pappou, what kept you going when things were that terrible?"

He didn't answer. He rinsed out the dishes and put them on the white rubber drain board. Then he went back into the dining room, to the table, and sat down. Yiayia and I returned as well.

Pappou finally answered me, "Ο Θεός πρώτα ('God first') and then family."

I knew pappou had donated his time, his money, and his heart to our parish, Zoodohos Peghe, in the Bronx. There were always Greek-Orthodox icons in the stores. There were pictures of Greek saints in the typical byzantine style above each register as reminders of his faith.

One of the proudest moments of his later years was Christmas Day in 1993, when he saw, in all its glory, the finished intricately carved, glowing wooden altar that he worked to have built for the church. In the early 1990s, when the altar was nearing completion, pappou took countless trips with my father to Astoria, Queens, to work with the Cypriot artisan who was sculpting the altar. With each new carving, my grandfather's heart burst with pride at the beautiful artwork he helped create. This was one way he contributed to the community.

I also remembered one very miserable, hot, humid summer day, a few years later, when no one seemed to know where my pappou was. The entire family, including my sister Christina and I, went searching for him, and then, we finally found him down on his hands and knees ripping weeds out of the church's garden. After his family, the church was everything to him and there was no task too small or too large that he wouldn't do for his faith or his family.

He said: "Perry, I am telling you these stories for a reason." Then he grew silent. He fidgeted with the rubber band awhile.

I honestly and enthusiastically told him. "I love these stories."

"This is who we are. It's very important," he said.

"Of course, I understand."

I waited for him to say more, but he sat there silently so I re-gathered my notes and put them in my bag.

"You're going?"

I had been there for hours at that point. No matter how long you stay, a real Greek will always act surprised when you get ready to leave. Fully aware of this attitude, I smiled and said, "We will do this again next week, okay?"

He nodded. "Tell me again why we are doing this, Perry?"

That session with pappou and yiayia had left me with more mysteries than understandings. It was clearer than even before that I was being given something more valuable than an oral history for my thesis, that I wasn't just doing this research for school. He knew that I am not one to make small plans, and he could feel my energy when we spoke that day. I thought about it for a moment.

"We have to share this story."

"Yes," he said, and he smiled. "This is bigger than you and me, Perrymou." Yiayia looked toward him in adoration.

I thought back to that day in Dr. Leichter's class when I was inspired to retrieve my uncle, Panayiotis' notebook. I remembered that the class was called "Family as Educator," and my professor was intent on getting us to remember how our grandparents educated us. Clearly I was being educated.

I looked at them both and in an attempt to keep them smiling said, "We will be bigger than John Stamos, you guys."

Yiayia widened her eyes and let out a big laugh. Pappou smiled at my audacity, and I packed up my things and kissed them goodbye.

I walked from my grandfather's house down Mickle over to my car. Instead of driving over to the highway and heading home, I decided to stay in the Bronx. I drove a few minutes and then stopped in front of the open-columned church steeple topped with a Byzantine cross. Zoodohos Peghe.

It was quiet inside the church and dark as well. Still, everything was familiar. The smell especially reminded me of my childhood in the Greek Church. I only half understood what was going on, but I fully understood that it meant something. I looked down at the marble floor as I walked over to the stack of candles at the right side of the entrance. I placed my two single dollar bills in the box and took a candle.

At the front of the church, there is a main door before the nave and on each side of the door, beautiful Greek iconography and two areas for lighting candles. The candles are white and they're traditionally placed into a small layer of sand to keep them standing. I made my "sign of the cross" and kissed the icons, lit my candle and then walked back into the empty church and took a seat. I found myself gazing at the altar pappou donated and praying for pappou, yiayia, my mother and my father, Christina, Giuseppe, and Elizabeth. I said a quick prayer for all of us.

CHAPTER 3

A Terrible Furnace

"And fate? No one alive has ever escaped
it, neither brave man nor coward, I tell you, it's
born with us the day that we are born,"
—**Homer,** *The Iliad*

It really is true that one of my clearest, early memories was walking between the stores in Inwood with pappou and my dad, just the three of us, together. I always wanted to work with my father and my grandfather. On the weekends, I would wake up with my father very early in the morning, excited to go to work. On some days, pappou would come to our house, walk our dog, and then we would all leave together. I was told that when my father was a kid, he didn't have a choice about working. Pappou would take him to work every day that he wasn't in school, and if he didn't wake up, he would get a cold, wet towel to the face and yiayia would employ the ever-present Greek guilt.

As we were walking from store to store, people from the neighborhood often shouted out a greeting to pappou. When they spoke to us, pappou and my father would introduce me. I shook everyone's hand, and they would say nice things about my father and grandfather. It made me proud, and pappou enjoyed presenting me as his "grandson who worked hard." Our interactions put an extra bounce in his step, and I saw him look so proud and happy as we walked from store to store.

I learned a lot about life and work in those stores. I cleaned the floors, wiped the tables, worked the register and went along to carry things on deliveries all over the neighborhood. My father's pizzerias were small stores, each with four or five rectangular tables, the classic white tile on the walls, and a baseball bat under each counter.

My father took great pride in making pizza. To this day, he will make pizza at home from scratch and enjoy the whole process. He opened the first store with a partner from the neighborhood, John's Pizza, and the second by himself and named it P. J.'s.

In those days, people shortened my name from Perry Joseph to P. J., so he would sometimes also call me P. J. I remember the night he thought of the name for his first pizzeria. I was eight years old, and we were sitting at the kitchen table in the Bronx. He was sketching the front of the store on a napkin and turned to me and showed me the finished product with my initials on the sign.

We employed people who lived in the neighborhood to help us run the stores.

There was Ralph, a local African-American man, the one-armed delivery guy/mechanic for the laundromats. He was hilarious and a very efficient mechanic. I would spend hours with Ralph and my father riding in the backseat as we picked up parts on Fordham Road. There was Teddy, a middle aged Greek immigrant who was very talented at making pizza and who refused to stop smoking while he prepared the food or acknowledge that customers couldn't understand him because of his accent. The third mainstay of the crew was Abe, a Mexican immigrant, who was our closest confidant and most efficient pizza man. We all "did our best with what we had" and that was where I started learning what that phrase meant. This was our work family.

My pappou was known for improvising to save a dollar. He made dustpans out of old cardboard box tops. He would always try to do jobs such as painting and repairs on his own rather than hire anyone.

Pappou believed there was a specific way to do everything, and everything was a science and an art with him. At each new store he counted his time spent there and then the time it took to travel between each store to make sure he was spending his time and energy as efficiently as possible. He could tell you how many steps it took him to get from one store to the other. Those stores were his art, his masterpiece.

After the stores were closed for the day, he would sit counting quarters from the laundromats with a precise system. The machine to roll the quarters was in front of him. To his left was the bag full of quarters, and to his right, small stacks of quarters rolled up in sleeves. Left, right, left, right. The guy was meticulous. We would sit there for hours counting quarters. I would usually pass out and leave my father and pappou at the table speaking Greek and shuffling the quarters into sleeves. (Quarters have an interesting, unique smell—a realization only reached after touching hundreds and thousands of them in succession.)

Despite his focus on efficiency, pappou would still entertain himself by making up little songs in Greek/English about the customers. I would hear him singing to himself, and I was laughing at the things he was singing about: "Old Rita does the πλύση ('washing'), but it isn't always hers...why does Selma always χαμόγελο ('smile') when she has to walk a μίλιο ('mile')..." All the women loved pappou. He was generally warm and kind with everyone. Women would come into the laundromat, hugging and kissing him, and he would always make them laugh. He had great charisma and, language barrier considered, a way with words.

But for all the singing and hugging, both my father and pappou were fiercely disciplined. There was no being late; there was no wasted time. The few occasions my pappou was stern with me were when I was messing something up. He would not tolerate messing up. There was the right way to do things—his way of doing things. Sweeping, painting, packing the trunk, wiping the tables, there was a precise methodology for all of these tasks.

When I visited his home, that same painstaking attention to detail was a characteristic of his actions there as well. He was methodical, focused, and relentless. When he made baklava, he had a system that demanded exactitude and elegance. Each cut created a perfect diamond. All the diamonds were displayed in precisely the same way.

His fridge was another example of organization and discipline. For one thing, there were always two fridges. One for American food and the other exclusively for extra orange juice and things he bought from a Greek grocery store in Astoria, Queens. Everything was in lines and the Greek fridge was almost always full of walnuts, yogurt and cheeses. It was a biweekly tradition to go to the Greek grocery after church. My aunt usually took both him and yiayia after service. Sometimes his habits made me crazy, but mostly it made me want to be just like him.

Now, my family no longer has pizzerias and laundromats. My father has a real estate brokerage firm. Dad is a broker with two offices in the Bronx where he sells homes, rents apartments and invests in real estate. But I miss the pizzerias and my dad does, too.

This was the work ethic I was raised with. People like my grandfathers went through an enormous amount of pain and suffering, but they were never defeated. Their lives were defined by their commitment to their family, their craft and their faith. My Italian grandfather also found it funny that people would sometimes say they had to "find themselves." We were joking about that one day, and Giuseppe said, "I would tell them to look in the sink." Although this may sound harsh, what I realize now is that he was right. He was in the construction business and he built magnificent structures with great pride and effort. He was really telling me to not search for an identity, but to make one.

This was just like he made his work and like he made himself. You can go to a number of locations in the Bronx today from the stairs of St. Raymond's church to the bulkhead extension into the water he built on City Island. We don't look for things, we make with what we have.

As such, I have never wondered who I was. In my head and my heart, I was both of my grandfathers, and I still am. I was fortunate to have them as role models, and essentially as builders for me to help construct an identity. I've always understood that with my name came strength, and most importantly, a list of obligations.

I was thinking about his powerful ethic the day I visited pappou near the end of October to hear his next story. I was preparing my thoughts as I walked toward the door when I was jarred by the sound of their television with the volume turned up astonishingly high. I walked up the stairs and entered the living room where I greeted yiayia first. She stood up and briefly explained that they were watching a Greek comedy show.

The show was the sort of comedy where a man in traditional Greek garb was walking around the streets pranking people. The appeal of these Greek television shows has always baffled me, but pappou was laughing so hard he was almost in tears. He waved me over to sit next to him, and he explained the show to me. I smiled along with his narration, but I still didn't get the humor. The mood was totally contrary to what I was expecting, but I was refreshed by the light heartedness. I sat and smiled along with them as they exchanged a few Greek phrases and hand gestures in response to what was happening on the show.

Then, abruptly, pappou picked up the remote and turned off the TV. Then he slapped me on my knee and stood up. He turned to yiayia. "Έλα, Mollie."

I walked over to yiayia, put my had on her shoulder, and repeated my grandfather's invitation: "C'mon, yiayia." She looked up at me and grabbed my hand. I helped her out of her chair, and we all walked to the table in the next room. They sat down, and I went back to the refrigerator to bring them some grapes. I put the grapes in a small bowl, walked back to the table, and took a seat across from pappou.

After he went through his normal routine of straightening his back, looking me in the eyes, and laying his palms flat in front of himself, he opened the book and asked: "Που είμαστε ('Where were we')?"

I checked my notes and answered: "You were in the mountains building the camouflaged pyramids to hide from the bombs…" He found the page he was looking for.

***

The Third Story:

We spent the winter of 1942 and most of 1943 in the mountain caves. Thousands of Greeks died of hunger. Hitler took everything because he wanted to starve us out. My father and Panayiotis and I made trips from our caves to nearby towns to collect food for our family. We made three trips to one town, Paramythia that was to the west, just south of the Albanian border, near the sea and the island of Corfu. The terrain was very difficult and the walk took six days there, and six days back. We crossed over wild rivers that were known for swallowing up everything.

The first day we walked for hours over high mountain passes and through fierce river currents. We carried our bags with our items for trade on our backs when we climbed, or on our heads when we waded through the water. We continued for two days until we reached the isolated house of a man named Gianni.

Gianni was an old man with white hair who always wore a vest, and he walked with a little hunch in his back. He was a very kind man who was willing to put us up for the night when we passed by his house. Then we woke up early the next morning and began walking again until we made it to our final destination. In Paramythia we traded our goods for cooking oil.

We always made trips like this, the three of us, and we would always take the same route. Nazis blocked the main roads so we had to take dirt roads that were more difficult. Those hidden paths were also patrolled by bandits who killed people traveling with goods to trade. Luckily, we never met any bandits, but a few times we walked by bodies on the path, men that had been killed and robbed. They lay rotting on the ground with their pockets turned out and all their belongings gone.

Those long days walking through the mountains with heavy weight on our backs would leave us dazed. We couldn't hear the normal sounds of the forest because of the gunfire in the distance. As we walked, and as our feet hit the ground, we could feel the tremors in the earth shaking from bombs and artillery fire. We couldn't hear birds, because they had all left the woods. I wondered where they went. Where could they go since the war was happening all over Europe?

When the Italian government surrendered to the Allies in the fall of 1943, the Germans not only sent several divisions into Italy to hold onto that country and continue the war, they also sent around 10,000 more soldiers into Greece to take over the occupation of the Italian zone in Greece. The Germans even attacked the Italian garrisons and killed or took many Italians prisoners. Many of these German soldiers had suffered through the fighting on the Eastern front against Russia. They were mean and angry and they didn't believe the Italians had been brutal enough to the Greeks so, like dogs in frenzy, they took out their revenge on Greece. That was also the time when they gathered up all the Jews in Thessaloniki and sent them to Auschwitz. They spared no one. They searched the mountains for partisans and killed any that they found.

The Andartes warned the Greeks to stay out of the villages because the Nazis were moving through them at such a rapid pace. Greek life came to a standstill and all the villagers were forced to flee into the mountains to try to survive like we were. The Nazis passed through Lagka and Nestorio many times, but they found no one because the villagers and guerrillas were in the mountains. Since they couldn't find anyone to kill, they burned whatever remained to the ground. The sign of terror, the swastika, fell over all of northern Greece. Over 25% of Greece's natural resources were destroyed along with roughly 10% of the population. Hundreds of thousands were killed or died of starvation.

While the Nazis were trying to subdue the northern part of the country, the Andartes constantly attacked them and mangled them. The Nazis had no chance against the *Andartiko* who were classic guerrilla fighters. They knew the territory far better than the occupiers. There were battles during which dozens of Nazis were killed and not a single Andarte was even injured, but these fights set the mountains ablaze with fire and the land flowed with blood. The Nazis were furious. They were outflanked, outsmarted, and outfought, so they turned to killing whatever innocent civilians they could find.

Near Nestorio, they found and slaughtered innocent people including women, children and the elderly. The enraged wolves followed the signals from the mouth of the beast, Goebbels, and the teeth of the beast, Himmler's S.S. troops, ripped apart entire generations. Hitler's orders were to spare no one. These were the orders and the achievements of Europe's most "civilized" leader who claimed to teach the world about progress and culture. Hitler's "civilization" was to use bayonets to extract babies from pregnant women in Kleisoura and then light up the ovens and burn them. Then they threw old people, women, and infants into the ovens as well.

As the terror got worse, we spent all of our time hiding in the mountains, and we couldn't even leave to make trips to Paramythia to find food or trade for supplies. We had to create even more of our own caves and the pyramid-shaped huts in the forests. We made everything so that we could stay indoors all of the time. We made a whole new village of pyramid huts in the forest. We even made ovens so we could bake bread when flour was available.

We had to live like animals in order to survive. We wouldn't have made it if not for our pyramids. We created ways of surviving, but our family was so large with our five younger brothers and our parents that my brother and I had to find another way to get food.

We knew we had to find work, which would mean leaving the mountains. In the early summer of 1943, Panayiotis and I decided to leave together, the two of us, and find work where the Andartes had set up their camp and a farm near Lagka. We thought we could earn wheat and bring it back to our family, but we never brought them the wheat. Our father, our mother and our brothers, were back in the caves waiting for us to bring them food and we never did. We wanted to bring them bread, and instead, all we brought them was anxiety, despair, and fear.

Our trip into darkness began the day we left the mountain. One Monday morning, very early, when fog still covered the mountain, we began our descent, and we reached the farm in less than an hour. Then we worked for another hour, and around that time, we saw soldiers arranging canons in the distance.

The workers around us started to look agitated, and then the sky was moaning as aircraft were circling above us. It seemed like the sun had vanished. I turned to my brother, and we shared a glance. We knew something terrible was going to happen. All we could do was wait and gather grain. Then everything was silent.

The wheat blew in the wind, and for a moment my mind drifted. There was quiet for a few minutes on that Andarte farm with my brother in the space between the wheat. It was the first time I heard it so quiet in a long time. The wheat was swaying back and forth in the breeze, and it reminded me of our farm back home. I could almost hear my mother singing.

Another hour passed. Workers around us started to leave. We thought maybe they had collected enough wheat. Suddenly, the Nazis opened fire on all those working in the fields. Shots rang out and people a few yards away from us began dropping to the ground. We started running when the Nazis turned their machine guns toward us. Bullets ripped through the wheat only a few feet away from us. A man called out to us from the distance, "Children, get down on the ground and crawl into that ditch!" He held his arm out and pointed to the right.

We ran and did exactly what he said. When we reached the ditch we were met by five people; three were wounded and two were dead. The whole farm shook as the bullets rained above our heads. Still holding our pitchforks and sickles, we ran into a ravine a few feet from the ditch. From there, we took off running. In the distance we could see the fires that were burning everything in their path.

The Nazis collected hostages as they passed through the fields. As we ran, we could see crowds of people being rounded up. Now more than ever, the sky blackened. The cannons groaned, and the Stuka bombers ripped through the air. As we tried to escape the fighting, we could hear the hissing gunfire as the Andartes fought the Nazis. Death's symphony accompanied us on our walk—the smell of fire, smoke, and red hot iron was everywhere. We walked through the night with a small group of people toward the nearest village. When we arrived there, we heard the news that the Germans had advanced, and they were entering nearby villages.

So, we were forced to leave and walk on to the next village in another direction. There we ran into an acquaintance of mine, a man named Konstanitos, from the café where we worked in Argos, and he helped us find shelter in a school. We slept for about two hours. Then, at around midnight, many others were arriving from the surrounding villages and they said that the Nazis were approaching. When we heard this, we left as the day broke. We decided to leave again toward the east, but that plan fell to pieces when we discovered that the Germans were battling around the Orlia Gorge.

We didn't know where to go as we began to walk randomly searching for some kind of cover. We learned from members of our group that the Germans had gone to Lagka and burned everything: the school, the church, and the rest of the village was totally destroyed. We were told that they took the elderly who could not or would not leave their homes up into the mountains and executed them. They rattled off the names of those who were executed: "Old Giorgios, Dimitrios and his wife Sofia, Aris the barber, Stefanos and his sister Maria, Ioannis and Eleni, Alexandros, Demetra…" Panayiotis and I recognized every name. As they shouted out these names, we stared at each other. In my mind, I could see all of their faces and the front doors of their homes. I knew Panayiotis could too. We kept walking. We made it to the mountains above the village of Avgerinos. From there we could almost see the battle lines, but the smoke obscured our vision.

We found another group of wandering people who warned us the Germans were approaching the mountains so we walked deeper into the forest. Shells from the canons were dropping down into the forest. Their machine guns were mowing down the trees and the bullets began to flutter by us. We dropped down to the ground and started to crawl. The bullets ripped into the tree trunks, the air was hot, and everything was teeming with smoke. I just focused on the dirt in front of me and kept moving forward. We decided to go to Zoni, and from there we would go to Ondria. We were familiar with that area, and it would lead us back to our village. Again, our plan was blocked by a battle that was raging in the area between the Germans and the Andartes. We constantly crawled between dangers.

When we moved toward a ravine in Avgerinos, we saw an entire side of a mountain that had lost its trees to the fires. There were hundreds of animals being herded by a group of Nazis right in front of us. Night fell and we could not move forward. We were trapped in the woods. We slept for a couple of hours and when we woke up Panayiotis told me he had a dream. He woke up and said, "I had a dream. The two of us were eating out of a sack full of sugar." I told him to not believe in dreams because they meant nothing. He heard that, looked at me and said, "Today the Germans will capture us."

***

With that sentence, my pappou lowered his head. He was exhausted. Yiayia's slim fingers gripped his wrist, and she was crying silently. My body was rigid from the tension I carried after listening to this story. I knew what came next, but I also knew we would not hear that part of the story on that afternoon.

I stood and carried the grape bowl to the refrigerator. When I returned to the table, yiayia asked me if I would mind bringing them a bowl of grapes. I was momentarily confused. I started to tell her I had already brought grapes, but I noticed pappou shake his head in order to tell me not to say more, so I didn't. I went back for the grapes and then sat down with them before it was time for me to go.

I turned toward pappou. "You and Panayiotis must have been terrified."

Pappou nodded in agreement.

"You could have died."

Again he nodded, but then he said: "It was bad. We couldn't get back home."

"To your family."

"They had no food. They had nothing. We couldn't get back to them. We couldn't help them."

I knew how devoted pappou had always been to taking care of us, how his hard work, his attention to detail, his obsession with doing everything exactly the right way was intended to make certain his American family was safe and secure.

Yiayia leaned toward pappou. "He always felt he and his brother abandoned their family in Lagka. But what could they do?"

Pappou patted her arm. Yiayia smiled.

"You didn't abandon them," I said.

"There must have been a way to get back," he said sadly. "There is always a way to fix things."

Yiayia added one of the phrases she was most fond of, "Where there's a will, there's a way."

That remark was typical of both their attitudes. I smiled, nodded and chuckled to myself.

Asserting our will in the face of chaos and misfortune with faith that we are acting correctly or that we will win is an important philosophical point. When I was a small child, I heard over and over again the story about the time my pappou and my father were driving home from work and their car caught on fire. They were on the Henry Hudson Parkway, so it took some time to pull over to the side of the road. Meanwhile, the fire was growing rapidly.

When they were finally able to jump out of the car, there were still bags full of quarters in the back seat. Pappou yelled for my dad to get the money. My father briefly hesitated. After all, the car was becoming engulfed in flames. But pappou yelled, "Πάμε!" ("let's go!"), and so they both ended up jumping back into the car and grabbing every one of the bags of quarters. Luckily, they weren't seriously burned. My father came home that night with no arm hair and a story to share.

That was my pappou. He ignored risk and always moved forward if he believed in what he was doing. The belief had to be there. He viewed all he had done as a prelude to doing more and helping our family build on his accomplishments and go on to greater achievements. He lived for the rest of us to be successful.

I know that he always wanted to do more, to be more successful himself, to start more businesses, to leave us with opportunities to go even further than he was able to go. But he never talked to me about his dreams. I never heard him say, "I want to do this." Instead, he always encouraged *our* dreams.

I would say, "Pappou, I got nominated for valedictorian."

He would say, "Do it."

"Pappou, I got into Columbia."

"Do it."

"Pappou, I'm going to write a book."

"Do it."

He always said, "You're the best." There was never any context or qualifier on that statement. He would just tell me I was the best. That was his "go-to" line with my sister Christina and me. He put his whole being into what he believed in, and family was certainly something he believed in.

I watched pappou and yiayia sitting across from me eating grapes. I studied the way my pappou was looking at yiayia. His gaze was uncharacteristically soft, unusually concerned. I realized he was worried about her although I was still not conscious of how concerned he was.

But I was suddenly aware of the obvious—that they were both aging rapidly. There was no amount of will power that could stop time. They were dependent upon each other, and they were becoming more wrapped up in each other. At the same time they were less involved in the world around them. In some ways, it was sweet, even romantic, to see them so close after all those years, but something was also troubling me, although I couldn't yet put my finger on it.

Pappou reached over, picked up the controller and turned the TV on. Greek TV. Another comedy. The volume was almost unbearably loud, but I sat there and watched the show with them. I made yet another attempt to follow the humor, but even with pappou and yiayia's descriptions and translations, the meaning escaped me. I sat with them for a few minutes just enjoying that they were so engaged.

Eventually I realized it was time to leave, but I still found it difficult to walk out of the door and be on my way. That day's story had been particularly gripping, but I sensed it wasn't just the story that was weighing on my mind. "Are you going to be okay?" I asked both of them.

They each looked at me as if I'd asked the most bizarre question imaginable. "Yes," my grandfather said gruffly. He was annoyed. "We are always okay."

And so I left them sitting there watching Greek TV with the volume so loud I could still hear the show three houses away as I walked down Mickle Avenue.

As much as I wanted to be like my pappou, I fully understood that he was forged in a terrible furnace. I would never, no matter how difficult things might become, ever experience that fire. Yes, I worked hard and tried, as he did, to be my best. In those ways, I was like him. But I had never starved, never ran through the woods pursued by Nazi soldiers, I never felt the desperation of believing I had failed my family. I could only ever try to emulate his kind of strength.

As my father once said to me, "You could stop doing everything else you do right now, and just work every minute for the rest of your life, and you still wouldn't work as much as pappou did."

And I knew that was true, but I also knew that I had to try. I smiled as this thought crossed my mind.

CHAPTER 4

No Sack Full of Sugar

*"Moral excellence comes about as a result
of habit. We become just by doing just acts, temperate
by doing temperate acts, brave by doing brave acts,"*

—**Aristotle,**
Classical Greek Philosopher and Scientist.

My pappou was not a formally educated man, but he was a voracious reader. When he grew older, it was common to find him at home with a stack of newspapers, and he skimmed each page quickly as he worked his way through the pile. In summer, I would find him sitting in a white undershirt, wearing παντούφλες (slippers), and reading a number of Greek and American papers. He was very smart, but never arrogant about his intelligence.

Pappou always encouraged all of us to get a formal education. As a result, both my father and his sister, Barbara, went to college. After college, my father started working on Wall Street; he worked his way up from the mailroom. He eventually became an analyst working in government securities. At that point he was able to help a number of other Greeks find jobs at Morgan Stanley.

His most notable and notorious hire was his best friend, also one of my uncles, Paul. The man was a legend. He was, at most, 5'9," and hovered around 300 pounds during his short life. He lived everything beyond the fullest and died in his thirties. He was a Greek-American with tough Spartan parents, but he was also a warm, kind-hearted man who was always the life of the party.

Men like my father and Uncle Paulie rose through the ranks. They did not have well-positioned parents and golfing on Saturdays connections. They had to work their way up.

My father always speaks fondly of his time on Wall Street. He was one of the "borough guys," and they had their own way of seeing things. One of the "chosen ones," a man not from the feta cheese crowd, once asked my dad what he did on the weekends. My dad, of course, replied: "I work with my father."

"Doing what?" The other man asked.

"Laundromats," my father replied.

"You gotta get a life, Greek," the man scoffed.

What the others didn't understand was that my father did have a life, it was just another sort of life from theirs. And it was, at times, far more exciting than the life lived at golf clubs or on the tennis courts.

An example of this is a story I have been told many times about when pappou bought another laundromat, and he was the proud new owner of the business in the Inwood section of Manhattan.

He quickly discovered that the location had a problem. The store was formerly a gang hangout. To make matters worse, pappou was new to that part of the neighborhood and didn't speak English very well. When pappou decided to open his store, he almost immediately began to deal with break-ins and vandalism. It turned out that the authorities wouldn't help my grandfather, basically because pappou was an immigrant with a heavy accent, and Greeks were on the outside in that community.

Finally, pappou talked with his friend Harry, a Greek who was born and raised in Turkey—an upbringing that made Harry a very, very tough guy indeed. Harry, pappou and my father, a teenager at the time, stayed in the property overnight. My pappou and Harry smoked an occasional cigarette and calmly stood in the dark store, holding pipes and waiting. As expected, the vandals broke into the store and when they did, they got a surprise. As the story goes, my young father held his own, and the vandals did not leave with any money and they did not damage the store.

After the event, the police brought some of the thugs to pappou's house, as a way to have my grandfather identify them. This small interaction worried him, because now the gang members knew where pappou, yiayia, my father and my aunt lived. Yiayia answered the door and was greeted by the smiling thugs.

That's when my father urged pappou to try the "American way." They hired a fearless lawyer, and the lawyer and my grandfather and my father marched into the police station demanding action. As a result of this new approach, the problem with the vandalism and robbery eventually stopped. That was the life my father lived during his weekends when he wasn't at the stock exchange.

On Wall Street, the Greeks quickly distinguished themselves and became "the Greeks." Even at work on Wall Street, my father never forgot about the family businesses. For example, my pappou's only brother in America, my

Great Uncle Dmitri, we call him Jimmy, made fur coats for a living, and at one point his business was doing very well. Anyway, my father ended up selling fur coats made by my Great Uncle Jimmy to his co-workers. I recently met one of my dad's old friends from Wall Street and he mentioned that he still treasured the coat he bought for his wife. The memories were always good when it came to remembering a deal from the "Greek guy."

On Wall Street, my father had a sense of belonging, but there was also a sense of being slightly different. I inherited this ability to blend while also feeling like an outsider. We embrace this feeling of being caught between cultures and maintaining or changing parts of each thoughtfully and confidently. This ability also goes beyond culture and into my personality and habits. I would often walk into class whipping my *komboloi* (Greek "worry beads") wearing an undershirt after a shift as a waiter, drinking a frappe. I would throw my keys with *il corno* attached ("the horn"—an Italian amulet) onto the desk in front of me and generally enjoy my classes without complaint. I enjoy the small ironies of life like listening to Salvador Dali interviews while lifting weights, studying Plato during the week at college and then helping my father do flashing on a roof on Saturday afternoon. We are Greek and Italian Americans who don't forget who we are but are obsessed with making progress. We strike our own type of balance. I am the first person in my family to get a degree from an Ivy League school, and I still keep a number of our traditional values and priorities. I see all of these things as connected because they're what I did for so long and I still think they're good.

This sense of marching to our own beat is something I inherited at a very young age. My mother, a professor, prioritized education. She wanted my sister and me to attend the highest-ranking elementary school possible. I was having difficulty reading, so I spent most of my early years in school sitting for hours with my mother at our dining room table practicing how to read. I would only have time to play with the kids in the neighborhood after studying and displaying a good effort and some progress for the day.

My high school experiences were more of the same. I focused on studying, sports, a few friends and, of course, my family. As the years passed, my friends started focusing more intensely on partying, drinking and eventually drugs; I did not. My senior year was characterized by push-ups, writing and working on the weekends when I could have been hanging out. When I was with my friends on the weekend, like many high schoolers, I felt different, and at school I felt the same way. I had the habit of walking the halls with my headphones on, blasting music when I felt like I needed some space.

That walking and thinking that often got me into trouble, ironically, influenced my work as a Philosophy Professor years later. I never sit when I teach, and I often give my students a set of questions that confront the broad themes of our work for that class. I put them in pairs, and we go outside and take a walk on the campus for ten to fifteen minutes. As they talk in pairs, I speed walk around and drop in on their conversations. I also play music in class when they do group work or individual work because silence bothers me. Teaching a 9:00 am Friday course requires that I walk in with energy and that they move around to get their minds going.

When I've asked them, all my students say that they never walk or even get up in class. I've seen many confused faces on students and faculty as they sit on the quad and witness a group of 30 people walking in pairs trying to answer questions like, "How do you make meaning on a daily basis?" (I often teach Existentialism.)

This feeling of being different, of course, applies to how I view my family. Personally, I like the fact that my parents and grandparents had back-yard gardens, that my father stood out on Wall Street for working at the laundromats, and that I was an odd student and am now a unique professor.

***

When I arrived at pappou's house the following week for our scheduled interview, my aunt was there, and she prompted me to go outside because pappou wanted to show me something.

He spent hours in his yard as he read or sat and talked with yiayia. He had a deep connection to nature, and, as with all things in his life, the garden was meticulous. The ground was furrowed neatly and all the vegetables were in perfect rows. He would place the hose at the top of each row; switch on the hose and in moments everything was irrigated. There were tomatoes, corn, and peppers, but his crowning achievement was his peach tree. I remember he actually videotaped the first peach that grew on this tree, and in the video he is holding his first peach, beaming with pride.

I went outside and my grandfather was eating a peach from that year's harvest. He held up a peach for me to examine while he told me about the peaches that grew on the family farm in Greece. I knew the peaches reminded him of home. He had grown something in his back yard in the Bronx that was close to all that he had left behind.

Then he cut the peach in half. We sat and ate it. Then I asked if he wanted to get to work and he said: "Ναι, yes, Perry." We walked upstairs and took our positions at the table. I heard my aunt leave. The fall sun breached the window shade and created a bright spot on the dining room table next to pappou's right side. Yiayia came in and sat by my side. And so, pappou began.

***

The Fourth Story:

All through that night in the summer of 1943, when we were trapped on the mountainside and Panayiotis had his sugar dream we huddled together to try and keep warm. We could hear Hitler's howling dogs search the mountain, rock after rock, tree, after tree, after tree.

When the sun rose, the slaughtering began again. The machine guns continued and the earth quaked. They poured bullets and bombs into the forest because they had already burned the villages. There was no thought and no humanity. The Nazis fired into the woods because they were getting hammered by the Andartes in the mountains as Greece tried to protect her sons and daughters.

At dawn, my brother, Panayiotis and I ran away from the woods where we were sleeping because machine gun fire was ripping through the forest. We headed for a ravine, then we rolled down a slope and ended up on a tiny road. We saw bodies everywhere, thousands of people, women, and children. They were all left in the dirt while wild animals skittered over their bodies. The animals were running from the hissing machine guns just like we were.

The Nazis occupied all the highest points on the hills. They sat perched like vultures, watching and waiting. If they saw anyone make the slightest move, they blasted them away with their gunfire. We stopped here and there to turn back while we were running, but there was no place we could go. The dirt beneath our feet was soaked red with blood and the sky above us was gray with smoke from the guns.

We did not have families, small children, or old folks with us, so we ran as fast as we could. As the two of us were running, someone yelled out to us and asked if we were alone. "I am also alone!" he yelled at us. "Follow me, and we can go towards Grevena. I know the area well." We stopped running to speak with him for a moment, and we explained that we had just come from Grevena. We told him that there were Nazis there.

He introduced himself as Giorgos and said, "I am from Anthiro in Kastoria. That is my village; I am a political executive in our party. If the Germans find me, they will skin me alive." We both knew that political executives of ELAS were the most wanted of the resistance fighters by the Germans. We continued to walk with Giorgos for a while, but when he insisted on going toward Grevena, we left him.

Where could we have gone? There was no place we could have gone. We began wandering in every direction. We passed a small field that looked like it had been a garden once, green and full of life. Not anymore. Ash covered everything.

Next to that field was another ravine where there was a small stream. We ran to the water and knelt down to take a few sips. I stopped for a moment, and looked at my brother. We were both exhausted. I saw his back shiver as he put his hands to the water. I also dug my hands into the water and frantically tried to quench my thirst. After a few gulps of water, we saw an old willow tree with long branches that reached to the ground

I turned to Panayiotis and told him that we should go lay under the tree. We could use the rest and the leaves would protect us from being seen. He looked back at me and nodded. We walked over to the tree and laid down, our heads were against the bottom of the trunk.

Next to the tree there was a thick, stone wall. Beyond this wall we could hear the guns firing in the distance and the cries of the innocent as Hitler's troops covered our land in death. Then, as we lay there, we heard another hissing. Not bullets this time. We looked to our right, and we saw it. A snake. A viper. It stretched itself out by our heads and then moved toward my brother.

I opened my eyes wide in shock. He returned my expression. I whispered, "Don't move, it will go away."

The viper gazed at both of us with its cold, black eyes. At any moment it could have struck us, and we would have been killed. We stayed totally still as the snake arrogantly stretched out in front of us, staring. As we lay there trying to be calm, but feeling frenzied inside our heads, we heard men approaching. When they came closer, we heard them speaking German. We could also hear that they had pigs with them. They went over to the ravine and we heard them slaughter the squealing, screaming pigs. Then they walked away from us.

For the next few hours, we stayed under the tree with the snake while the Nazis started a fire and roasted the pigs. Sometimes we could feel their footsteps only a few yards away from us. The viper coiled itself up and made itself comfortable between us as beads of sweat formed on both of our heads. We exchanged glances, but never said a word. We were watching the snake and listening for footsteps.

Then we heard men approach our hiding place. Two soldiers walked directly across from our tree but did not notice us. As their steps landed, the viper became agitated. It began to move about, writhing and jerking slightly. Our breaths became heavier, and, just as the soldiers passed our tree, the snake shot out from between us and slithered toward the soldiers who were only about ten feet away from the tree. The soldiers saw the snake and they only needed to follow its tail to see our feet. They walked towards the tree and lifted the branches.

They stared at us. Their uniforms had yellow ribbons, which indicated that they were unarmed. Greeks. Snitches. They let the branches fall back down and they walked away. For a moment, we thought they might take pity on us.

But, less than a minute later, before we could run away, the snitches returned with German soldiers. The soldiers lifted the branches and we stared down the barrels of their rifles. We did not move. There was a moment of strange calm and stillness that came over the both of us. We knew that we had entered the claws of the beast. I thought to myself, how did this happen? And then, why did this happen?

The soldiers yelled at us in German. Then the snitches yelled at us in Greek, "Get up!" They grabbed us at gunpoint. The black day had arrived and my brother's dream of eating sugar was false, but his premonition was right: we were captured.

We walked with the snitches and the German soldiers until we reached a large flat area where there were hundreds of people. We sat there for hours and every few minutes they collected more people. They didn't treat us like humans. They treated everyone like they were dropping coins in their pocket as they shoved them into the crowd. They would come, drop people off, leave, and then return. Their cold eyes never glanced at the bodies they dragged into the area. They turned to each other, laughed, and gloated about their success in capturing unarmed villagers. Meanwhile, the rebels were pounding them. They never captured any Andartes.

We recognized many people from our village in this group; their faces were thin from starvation, and their eyes wilted from exhaustion. Two men, Mallio and Manio, stood out though, because they were fat and well rested. They had two mules loaded with plunder. Everything from clothes to food was loaded onto their animals. They had taken these items from the villages that were burned. These men were snitches, traitors, so they were able to move freely and profit from our suffering.

The soldiers returned and forced us to start walking. They herded us like sheep. We passed by the tree that we were caught under. We continued to walk and they brought us to a small church. The German sergeant who caught us came back toward us. His name was Otto. He walked among the captives, the brave conqueror of children and old people—no one in the church was armed when they were captured. He pranced through the crowd of people sitting on the floor and his eyes were bouncing around, his nose slightly lifted as he sniffed through the groups. I turned to Panayiotis and told him that Otto was looking for us. Then he found us.

He took us and lined us up next to the mules that had been loaded with goods from the villages. He assigned five animals to my brother and five to me. The animals were lined up, all loaded with goods one after the other. He put me on the road to follow the path. I was 200 meters in front of Panayiotis in this line. Otto did this to put us out of contact, to separate us.

We headed for Pentalofos, each step monitored by soldiers who flanked us on both sides. In the afternoon we arrived at another small village, and Otto ordered us into his tent. He confiscated our identification cards and sent us away. As we walked out of the tent, we could see the Nazis torching the village. The soldiers set up camp outside the village and watched the smoke rise. As we walked away from the tent, we saw soldiers playing cards and laughing as the village burned behind us.

Very early the next morning, we loaded up the animals and continued toward Pentalofos. When we reached Pentalofos, a committee appeared and spoke in German to the officer in charge. That is how their village was saved even though the Germans did set up camp there.

Pentalofos was a small town where we were put to work digging holes. The holes were one and a half meters wide and one and a half meters deep. We would dig them five days a week, all day. With each shovel full of dirt, I felt that I was digging my own grave. They would take us out in small groups, far away from the encampment, to dig these holes. In our minds, every step we took away from the camp was a step towards our death. We walked, we dug, and we waited.

Soldiers who, at any moment, could have killed us, always escorted us. Panayiotis and I dug with our stomachs in our mouths; never sure of what was going to happen. One day, when we finished the holes, we saw the soldiers bring the food scraps they didn't want to eat. All the leftovers were thrown in these holes and covered with dirt so the garbage would not cause a stench that would disturb the camp. The Nazis were sophisticated animals.

We eventually realized that garbage was the only reason for our digging the holes and that we were probably safe for the moment. On these trips out to dig, Panayiotis and I were always separated. Otto somehow knew neither of us would try to escape if we were not together.

***

When he stopped talking, my pappou closed his eyes, and rubbed his hands across his face. He was not trembling as he had been at the end of previous stories. I saw a grimace, and then tension across his forehead. I realized he was sad. I said: "Did you plan an escape?"

He didn't answer at first. Then he said: "We always did everything together." He sighed and stared into the middle distance. "Otto kept us apart."

"Yes," I said. "He knew you needed each other."

I paused, looked and saw that pappou had eaten all the peach slices we put out in the bowl on the table. He closed the book. I asked him if he wanted more peaches, gesturing towards the empty bowl, and he nodded. I grabbed the bowl and went into the kitchen. Yiayia, as usual, followed me. She stood and watched as I sliced another peach. Then she wiped the counter clean where the sweet, yellow juice had spilled onto the tile.

When we returned to the table, yiayia said to pappou: "I was just showing Billy something I was cooking."

Pappou stared at her. I looked back and forth between the two of them. Yiayia frowned. "Of course, I mean Perry," she said. "I was showing... Perry. He was... cutting a peach."

I smiled and touched her hand and said, "Yes, that's right. I was."

I looked at pappou. He didn't want to look at me. He lowered his head, picked up a napkin and began folding it into smaller and smaller squares.

Yiayia frowned when she saw pappou folding the napkin. Nervous tics bothered her. She was constantly smacking my knee during our discussions because I would habitually shake my legs.

She turned toward me, pointed toward pappou folding his squares, and said: "Look at your father. He can't stop fidgeting." She still spoke as if I were my father, Bill. She was still confused.

Pappou smiled at her, then at me. Trying to ignore the obvious, he said, "She doesn't like it when I fold napkins." We shared a nervous laugh.

Of course neither of us were really thinking about nervous tics. I could see pappou was worried about yiayia, but I also knew he wouldn't say anything about her condition. Even to me. In that, he was just like my Italian grandfather, Giuseppe, who, when he became blind, went from building massive, elaborate and beautiful structures to not even being able to watch television or see his grandchildren but he never referred to his blindness. Never complained. He did his best to act as if nothing had changed. Then he developed a relationship with death that was very philosophical. He was a very bright man. To articulate it simply, he had an "I'm not dead yet" mentality.

I know he had a spinal tap as an adult and that was intensely painful. He fought in WWII, and he would sign up to drive trucks with nitroglycerin packed in the back because the job paid more. He was also a "sand hog," constructing tunnels deep underground, again, doing a dangerous job to earn extra money. Death was constantly around him, and it must have been such a constant consideration and possibility that it really didn't matter. The Stoics believed that to face death in one's mind every day is to fortify the mind, body and soul. Giuseppe woke up to darkness every day and still lived happily. Maybe the Stoics were right.

Neither of my grandfathers ever thought, "What if I die doing this or that?" or if they did, they were, like the Stoics, able to dismiss those thoughts quickly and move on to focus on what was in their control. The past was their teacher, the present their art and the future was an open question. They weren't "What if?" people. Near-death experiences didn't appear to bother either Giuseppe or pappou. There were only two things, life and death, "near" was not relevant. They simply didn't spend a lot of time on the "What ifs?" of life. That was a positive strategy for both of them, because once they reached the conclusion that life's consequences are inevitable, they were free to live and to love people passionately, because they weren't constantly thinking, "What if this ends?"

I'm also not a "What if?" person. It is the "What ifs" of life that drive people crazy. There is only one inevitability in life—that it will end. Understand this, feel this, and face it, and not much else will frighten you. Our freedom is in our awareness that we are finite.

However, when my pappou first glanced at yiayia and clearly saw her confusion, he did have a brief "What if" moment. He couldn't help it. But he was able to put aside that thought and pretend to joke with me. I went along with his pretense. What else was I to do?

It was late afternoon, and I knew they would soon begin preparing their dinner. I wanted to get home, but I also found that it was becoming more and more difficult to break the intimacy we created when pappou told his stories and yiayia and I listened with horror, sadness and admiration. I found myself lingering a little longer each time we met, and in the process I noticed that below the surface of their strong, confident lives, unavoidable decline was creeping in. I could see it. I could feel it. But I myself avoided the "what if." The looming reality was too much to contemplate.

"So, pappou," I said, "We have a lot of stories left?"

"Many more," he said. "We are still near the beginning."

"Good," I said. "I will have a great collection to present."

"Present?" asked my grandfather.

"Yeah, for my thesis."

"Ah, for school," he nodded. "Yes, and yours will be the best." He looked at me. "You're always the best, Perry." My yiayia added, "The best!"

That time, when I left them, I wandered over the few blocks to our old family house on Seymour Avenue. There was another family living there, eating there, sleeping there, fighting and loving there. My father and mother, my sister, and I, had moved out to the suburbs. We had a house in Westchester County, but I missed the old neighborhood. I missed our old house. A huge wave of nostalgia washed over me as I stood and stared at the brick semi-attached home, the trees that were taller, the white door, the window of my old bedroom.

Then there was movement behind the curtains on the first floor. Someone was peering out at me, and it was getting dark. I was a stranger, and I no longer belonged there. I slowly turned and walked away.

CHAPTER 5

God and the Evil Eye

"What we have in us of the image of God
is the love of truth and justice,"
—**Demosthenes**,
Athenian statesman and orator

The Greek Orthodox religion has been an essential element of Greek identity ever since the Great Schism of 1054, when the Greek Orthodox Catholics split from the Roman Catholics. The standard religious explanation for the split between Rome and Constantinople was the refusal of the Ecumenical Patriarch of Constantinople, Michael I Cerularius, to accept the papal authority of the Bishop of Rome, Pope Leo IX. However, like many such religious conflicts, the true battle was over complex issues of power and control between what was then called the Eastern Roman Empire, or Byzantium, and the Western Roman Empire, the nations of Western Europe.

Then, when Constantinople was captured by the Ottomans in 1453, Greek Orthodox Christians fell under the political control of the Muslim Turks, and while we were not allowed any expression of political freedom or national identity, we were generally allowed to practice our religious faith quite openly. As a result, the most powerful expression of our Greek identity was through our faith as Orthodox Christians. When large numbers of Greeks immigrated to the United States in the early 1900s, it was again the Greek Orthodox churches that were the centers for maintaining Greek identity.

Religion was a very important part of life for both pappou and Giuseppe, whose Italian identity in America was also closely associated with faith, in his case, the Roman Catholic Church. So, religious faith in God has always been an important part of my life.

Faith and religious tradition. Everyone in my family makes the sign of the cross when we pass a Greek Orthodox or Catholic Church. Even Giuseppe could tell by how our car moved and how the road felt when he passed the church he visited every Sunday, so he made the sign of the cross whenever we drove past his church. Minutes before he died, after battling a myriad of ill-nesses, Giuseppe asked my mother, "Where's my cross?" My mother gave him his cross and shortly thereafter, he passed away. In that moment of death, his faith was what mattered to him.

My family prays before we eat, and we pray before we go to bed. One of the first longer pieces I memorized as a very young child was the Lord's Prayer and the words, "Our Father who art in heaven…" I still pray every night, and I touch three small icons after I pray. One is a figurine of the Virgin Mary's face, another is a small statue of St. Joseph, and the third is a Greek Orthodox wood-paneled triptych, a portrayal of Jesus Christ on one side and the Virgin Mary holding the baby Jesus on the other.

I remember, when I was a child, noticing that Giuseppe had, in his bed-room, a statue of praying hands. Later I found out my mother actually made that statue for her parents. Hands held in prayer are important to us.

My dad also believes. To this day, he wears a cross that pappou found in one of our laundromats. The cross was discovered in one of the washing machines, and when pappou saw it, he posted a notice letting patrons know about the recovered item. When no one claimed it, pappou, who would never let anything go to waste, gave the cross to my father as a present. I have always found this story a somewhat humorous, instructive demonstration of how work, family and faith are so strongly connected in my family.

My father has often said that, "There is God, and so there is also the devil." To protect against evil, I have always worn a cross, and, in addition, I wear *il corno*, the Italian superstitious symbol to protect me from the evil eye. I wear them on two separate chains, as is the custom, because one is not supposed to wear them on the same chain. So in that sense, superstition has accompanied religion in my life and the life of my family.

When my dad was a child, there was a woman named Eleni, one of yiayia's friends, who was known for having prophetic and vivid dreams, and she would often telephone yiayia to share her revelations and premonitions. One morning when my father was heading out the door to go to school, yiayia warned him to be extra careful. When my father asked why, yiayia replied that Eleni had a dream that he would be hit by a bus and die that day. My father is said to have jokingly replied, "Thanks, ma. Ham and cheese for lunch today?"

However, in my family, dreams and the evil eye are things to be taken seri-ously. I remember an Easter gathering at my great uncle's house. One of the babies in the family would not stop crying. My second cousin and her husband tried everything to quiet the child and make him smile, but nothing worked.

Eventually, after a long period of uninterrupted crying and screaming, one of the older members of the family declared that the evil eye had been placed on the child.

A local Greek woman was called, and she came over to take the evil eye off the crying baby. She walked into the house, and with no introduction, no hesitation, she headed straight over to the baby. She had an evil eye with her, and she began mumbling prayers over the baby and making the sign of the cross. During this ritual, no one was allowed near the baby except for the woman performing the ritual. Christina, my sister, was thrown into a slight panic, but, as I calmly ate my food, I turned to her and said, "This is the 'Greekest' thing I have ever seen."

Surprisingly, or perhaps not surprisingly, the baby stopped crying, and he finally went to sleep. There is a chance that, among other ministrations, the woman just gave him a tiny sip of *ouzo*, but we'll never know. The woman left the adjoining room, and walked into the dining room where everyone was sitting. She walked over to my second cousin who invited her to join us. The woman declined, hugged both my great uncle and his wife, and then said goodbye.

I describe this anecdote a little casually, not because I don't believe in such things, but because I do, and they make me uncomfortable. One would think that after the kind of schooling I've received, I would be more logical, more rational, but that is not the case. I myself have prophetic dreams, and have, most certainly, been visited by the deceased. The most notable example of this was a dream about Giuseppe.

I was walking down the block near his old house in Pelham Bay. It was the street that we always would stroll down when I was a kid. I passed in front of my barber, a Sicilian and close friend. I stopped for a second and greeted him in Italian as I always do. Giuseppe suddenly approached from the other side of the street. He came over to me and we started speaking Italian together. He then began speaking in our dialect, which I do not understand. And although I knew that I didn't understand, I also immediately recognized what he was saying. We said goodbye and when we went to hug I was jolted awake. I was out of breath and in shock.

A psychic once told me that since I am the third generation in my family with this ability, I should embrace it, and the dream about Giuseppe has stayed fresh in my mind, so I think about it frequently.

There is a family friend of ours who is unbelievably accurate in her predictions. Her name is Lola and she is from Cyprus. She is a lovely woman who is humble, kindhearted and helpful. She often calls my house with news of a vision she's had. She predicted the exact town where I would hold my first job, my boss's background and on what date I would find out that the job was available.

Lola recently gave me a full reading along with a spiritual realignment. She used Greek Orthodox religious iconography in her rituals, and when she heard angels speaking, she relayed their messages to me. Among other things, she predicted I would write this memoir of my grandfather. I wrote another book before this one, and she randomly called the night I finished it and said "Perry wrote a book. He's going to write another one that people will love." As a result of my last meeting with her, I say certain prayers, a certain number of times every night, and I drink holy water before I go to sleep.

These superstitions are really a sort of "Oracle-at-Delphi" Greek tradition. I often think about that tradition, and about how people like me have been going to people like Lola for centuries to acquire some sort of affirmation or certainty. All of these things are very real to us. When my mom was pregnant, yiayia said she shouldn't hold any other children because it would cause her to miscarry. When my dad was just a kid and he would lie down on the floor, on his stomach, watching television, no one ever stepped over him because it would have stunted his growth. If you're saying something and someone sneezes, the sneeze means it's true and you have to say, "it's the truth."

The interior design in pappou's house reflected my family's tradition of mixing religion and superstition. Strange juxtapositions of visual representation of Greek gods and Christian iconography could be found everywhere. We still, thousands of years later, hold on to polytheism in a way that has always reflected the best of our culture. We also continue to name children after mythological figures and the ancient Greek gods. Then we baptize them in the Greek Orthodox faith.

Pappou believed that Panayiotis had an ability to tell the future and that he had visions. In an earlier story from the notebook, Panayiotis has the dream that he and pappou eat out of a bag of sugar. He tells pappou about it, and pappou says they should not believe in dreams. Panayiotis then said, "We'll be captured today." They were captured later that very morning.

On the day of my next visit with pappou, a visit that must have occurred around the beginning of November, Panayiotis had called from Greece and spoken with my grandfather. He predicted that Saki, the son of their brother, my Uncle Dmitri, was going to have some good luck.

Pappou was telling me about that conversation when I arrived at the house. Yiayia answered the door, and I went inside to sit next to my grandfather who was sitting on the couch. I noticed there was a dark brown, wooden walking cane next to him on his right side, leaning against the armrest. I thought that was odd because pappou had always refused to use a cane. Then, when it was time to begin our session, pappou reached for the cane and leaned on it heavily as we walked slowly toward the table.

I decided not to say anything about his cane, but pappou himself remarked, "I use the cane now, Perrymou. Yiayia insists."

I glanced over at yiayia and she nodded in agreement. Then she went into the kitchen and brought out a small bowl of dark green olives.

When we reached our usual positions—pappou across from me and yiayia next to me—my grandfather took a few deep breaths. He seemed tired from the brief walk. We waited. My right knee began shaking up and down in nervous anticipation. Yiayia slapped my thigh. Pappou sat up straight, opened the notebook, closed his eyes, opened them again and began to share another memory.

***

The Fifth Story:

After a few days in Pentalofos, our tired column of captured prisoners continued our sad march toward Florina. We only traveled on major roads at night so we could avoid the British aircrafts that would bomb us because they thought we were all Germans. We walked past a number of deserted villages. The buildings, the houses, the fields and orchards, the people had been swept away completely.

It was almost fall in 1943, when we stopped at a village that had become a German army station. We were allowed to walk freely in that village because there was an army division posted there and the village was heavily guarded. Panayiotis and I were walking through the village when we saw an old woman waving at us. We walked over to her, and she invited us into her home.

She was from North Epirus and she spoke Greek. She was a small woman who stood almost perfectly straight. She had long black and gray hair, and warm dark eyes. She didn't give us her name, but she asked where we were from. When we told her our story, she started crying. Then she told us that three weeks earlier the Germans killed her two sons along with another forty people in the public square. They also sent six guerrillas and another ten people to Germany where they were to be kept as hostages. She wept and her hands quaked.

I placed my hand on her shoulder. Her head lowered and she grabbed my wrist with her opposite hand. Then she forced herself to stop crying. She stood up even straighter, and noticed that my brother's shirt was ripped. She told him that she would fix it. We said she did not have to because his shirt was fine. She insisted, so we both gave in. While Panayiotis was pulling off his shirt, she offered us food. Again, we tried to refuse her. We told her that we were okay and that she needed the bread for herself. Again, she insisted, and she gave us the bread. We embraced her and thanked her.

We then told her that we had to leave and she began to cry again. She blessed us and wished us well. She said that she would pray for God to get us home safely. We thanked her and she stood by the open door as we walked away.

We rested for another day in that small village, then, as soon as it was dark, we left for Florina. By daybreak we had reached the village of Kleidi. There were beautiful apple orchards in that area, and we set up camp among the fruit trees for camouflage.

As soon as we arrived, they organized all forty of us, including a priest from Zouzouli, Father Thomas, into rows of four. While we were standing there, a German officer approached the priest, grabbed him by the beard, and punched him until the priest fell to the ground. Then the German started to kick the priest. As he beat him, he was screaming at the priest that he was an Andarte, a partisan, a rebel who killed German soldiers. Panayiotis and I pleaded with another officer to stop the beating. Father Thomas had been very kind to the both of us, and he was a good man. He was not a killer. We shouted and yelled, and finally the beating stopped, but the priest was nearly beaten to death. His body lay on the ground, motionless, except for his chest slowly heaving for air. We walked over and helped Father Thomas to his feet. He thanked us and limped along as we proceeded to Florina.

When we arrived at the district headquarters in Florina, we were marched straight to the prison where giant iron doors swung open. They threw us inside, and we were surrounded by barbed wire charged with electricity. They slammed the doors closed, and there we were, in the prison camp we had heard about for so long because all of our fellow villagers who were captured were sent to Florina or other places with detention centers just like that prison. We sat on the cold ground and waited with the priest, trying to make sure that he was okay.

A few hours after the gates closed, another German officer came over to us with an interpreter. The interpreter asked Father Thomas if he was an Andarte, and the priest replied that he was not. He said that he was just a priest, but the Germans treated everyone like an Andarte to heal their wounded egos after the great losses they had suffered.

The officer looked us over carefully, and spoke to the interpreter. The interpreter, another traitor, turned to us and said, "You're all going to Thessaloniki and then to the army camps in Germany. You are all guerrilla rebels." As he walked away, he scoffed at us like we were animals.

That night, an escort of guards took us to a large square in Florina. We slept there on the ground covered with a few thin blankets, and in the morning, we were escorted to the train station. We were herded into a train car like cattle, all stuffed together. Once we were all stampeded into the coach, they whipped us on our heads. We were bunched so close together that we could not even move our arms.

We were all afraid, because we were sure that we were going to Germany to be executed. Father Thomas said a prayer, but no one was able to make the sign of the cross since we were so close together. All we could do was stand and wait. In that moment, we were forced to practice the most powerful kind of faith—to be hopeful in a time of complete hopelessness. Faith was the only thing we had to hold on to in those moments.

The one window in the car was covered with barbed wire, but soon many of the prisoners were able to recognize where we were, and they assured us that we were, in fact, headed for Thessaloniki. This was a slight relief. When we reached Thessaloniki, we stood in the coach for a whole night, completely still before they let us out.

When they removed us from the train, we were hungry, covered in lice, and exhausted. They lined us up in the dirt, and then began beating us at random. They surrounded us with automatic weapons, and individual soldiers dove into the crowd kicking and punching anyone in their path.

Again, an officer stomped to the front of the crowd with an interpreter—another Greek traitor. I felt a boot slam into my stomach, and bent over clutching my belly in my hands. I looked up to see the Greek who had betrayed us all, who had betrayed himself to gain favor with those cowardly tyrants.

The beating continued for a few more minutes, but I avoided getting hit again. We began our walk through the town, and we heard people grumbling that they would slaughter us like lambs. The townspeople stared at us with pain and worry. There was nothing any of them could have done to save us.

So, we found that we had not escaped our biggest fear. We were captured in the nets of terror at the infamous army camp at Pavlou Mela in Thessaloniki.

***

This time, when he finished his story, my grandfather made the sign of the cross before he closed Panayiotis's notebook. His eyes were misty. That was unusual because my grandfather seldom showed physical emotion. Yiayia tapped me on the arm. "He is still very upset about the way the soldiers treated the priest."

I turned to pappou. "Was Father Thomas an Andarte?"

"Ναί, yes," said pappou, "Ημασταν όλοι αντάρτες."

"They were all Andartes," Yiayia translated. Then she added, "At least after they were imprisoned in the camps."

I nodded.

"But he was a καλός άνθρωπος," added pappou. "A good man. He never hurt anybody. He never carried a weapon. He was a man filled with *philotimo*. A man of integrity, love and kindness."

"Do you know what happened to him?"

"He died in the camp at Pavlou Mela. The Germans beat him all the time. One day he didn't recover, and he was dead." Pappou again made the sign of the cross.

I took two olives from the bowl, gnawed on the flesh, rolled my tongue around the pit and then spit out the pit and placed it on a napkin. "He sounds like he was a good man," I said. "It's a shame that he died."

"There were many who died," said yiayia quietly. "So many dead."

It was getting on toward dinnertime, and I asked them what they were going to eat that night.

"I'm not hungry," said pappou.

"He doesn't eat much anymore," said yiayia.

"I eat fine," argued pappou. He was annoyed. He rose from his chair and walked back to the couch without his cane, but he was unsteady on his feet, and I was afraid he would fall.

When he settled in, I continued our conversation about his earlier phone call with Panayiotis. "So, you were saying you talked on the phone with your brother?"

"Yes."

"He said Dmitri would get lucky," said yiayia.

"Not Dmitri," grumbled pappou, "Saki. He said Saki would get lucky."

"Yes, Saki," yiayia corrected herself.

"Did he say what would happen?"

"No," said pappou. "He only said he had a dream that good things would happen to Saki."

I asked them if they wanted me to turn on the television, and they both nodded yes. While they watched another Greek comedy, I wandered around their house, checking on things. Making sure everything was okay. I was beginning to seriously worry about both of them. It was a shock to realize to what degree things were changing. They had both always been so strong, so vital, so on top of things. They were the rocks upon which my family was built and it was painful to think that the foundation was crumbling.

But their house seemed fine. Everything was in its place, neat and orderly and precise. I decided that perhaps I was exaggerating my concern.

When I returned to where they were watching television, I found yiayia sitting alone in front of the TV. I asked about pappou. She looked around the room, seemingly unaware of his absence. Then she smiled, and said: "Oh, yes, that's right... he's getting ready for bed, Bi..., I mean, Perry."

It was still early evening, so I went toward his bedroom to make sure he was all right. When I approached his room, I saw that he had left the door slightly ajar and I caught a quick glimpse.

Pappou was kneeling at his bedside, praying. His back was to the door and he didn't know I was there. I stopped at the doorway and didn't enter the room while I watched him kneeling on the floor, his eyes raised in supplication. The last rays of the day's sun were shining in from a window that was opposite where he was kneeling. He appeared focused and at peace.

I thought back to the time when my father and I accompanied him to Astoria in order to watch the Cypriot woodcarver fashion the final touches for the Zoodohos Peghe altar—pappou's altar. I thought pappou would be excited and anxious to see the altar finished, but instead, he was quiet and contemplative, focused and at peace much like he was as I watched him kneeling in prayer. His God was his refuge and his strength when things were difficult. I also remembered he told me, "If we have faith, if we have love, things get better." But I failed to see how faith and love were going to make things better this time. Neither were our charms, dreams or superstitions.

I returned to the room where yiayia was watching TV. She was laughing about one of the sketches being played out on the screen.

"He's all right," I said. "I think he is getting ready for bed."

My yiayia had a perplexed look on her face. "Billy?"

"No, yiayia, pappou. Pappou is getting ready for bed."

She searched the room again. She said, "Oh...yes... okay."

I asked her if there was anything I could do for her.

"No," she said. "I'm fine, Perry."

When I left the house, I was somewhat depressed. It was becoming clear that yiayia's memory was failing, and my pappou was getting weaker. I didn't really know if there was anything I could or should do. I knew I needed to talk to my mother and father. And I promised myself to hurry along the process of recording all of pappou's stories while he could still tell them.

Then, during the following week, I heard the news that Saki, Dmitri's son for whom Panayiotis had predicted good fortune, received a significant raise at his work. That news put a smile on my face, and, at least for a while, Saki's good fortune lifted my spirits.

CHAPTER 6

No One Sleeps

"If you have no confidence in self, you are twice defeated in the race of life. With confidence, you have won even before you have started,"

—**Marcus Tullius Cicero,**
Roman Philosopher, statesman, orator.

M y pappou and my other grandfather, Giuseppe, really did become best friends. I imagine that such a very close relationship between fathers-in-law is extremely rare, and I believe they were so close because they had a true and robust respect for each other. They would call each other every day, and they would often spend time together outside of family gatherings which we had every Sunday. There are numerous pictures in our family albums of them with their arms around each other—broad, genuine smiles on both their faces.

I sometimes think of myself as the living member of the triumvirate composed of my two grandfathers and myself—pappou (Pericles), Giuseppe, and me—Perry Giuseppe. We are all bonded together, forever, with my name, and this gives me confidence. I accept the fact that it's a little strange to think that way, but I feel like I need to be brazen. If my mission in life is to make their struggles worthwhile with my work, there's not much room for sheepishness.

Giuseppe and his family settled in New York City, when he arrived as an infant in America. He was born in *Gioia del Colle* in Bari, Puglia, on a rather desolate plateau near the heel of the Italian boot. His father, Vincenzo, worked on New York construction crews, mostly in concrete, something Giuseppe ended up doing as well although Giuseppe had his own company. His mother, Rosaria was a teacher who died of leukemia when Giuseppe was just 23.

The company that Giuseppe ran with his brother, Nick, and eventually my cousin Frank and his brother was called Vacca Brothers, Vacca being their last name. They started out with one small green truck with that name on the side. Now that my Cousin Frank and his brother and his son run the business, Vacca

Brothers is responsible for restoration of some of New York City's landmark properties.

In addition to the construction company, Giuseppe was also part owner of club in Queens, New York, called "Yesterdays." He would work during the day on a construction site and then go check on the club at night.

My grandmother's brother, Vinnie, "Uncle Vinnie" we call him, met his wife, Grace, in that club. Giuseppe was with my grandmother at the time, and she brought her younger brother, Vinnie, to the club one night while visiting my grandfather. Vinnie was introduced to Grace, and they hit it off. She is an absolutely lovely woman who was also raised in Bari and came to America as a child.

The Vacca family first lived in Manhattan around 104th street, but after a few years they moved to the Bronx, to Castle Hill on Purdy Street in the Bronx, very close to where pappou and his family lived. His sister, Mary, recalls that the family said the rosary every night, and they went to church every Sunday. Giuseppe was very musical. He played the guitar and the mandolin, and I have vivid memories of him playing the guitar.

When I think about pappou or Giuseppe, I feel able to answer a question that has been asked by philosophers for centuries—what does it mean to be human? For me, because of them, being human means standing by the people and the ideas that you love in every way you can. My grandma Elizabeth and my mom stood by Giuseppe when he went blind. Giuseppe was by far my mother's most ardent supporter when she went for her PhD. One of his favorite things to say was "get 'em, Lisa." Yiayia stood by pappou when he needed help speaking English, and pappou stood by her when she became forgetful. My dad stood by pappou when he was in the hospital and I'm trying to stand by all of them by writing about them. They taught me to do what I can, as often as I can, for those I love, and then, when I die, I hope everyone I leave behind does the same.

It is easy to simplify my grandfathers because, in the eyes of the world, they appeared to be very simple men. They loved their work, they were committed to their families, they had faith in God and they lived each day in pretty much the same way. But those very facts made them, in my eyes, very complex. They were extremely intelligent and driven to succeed, but for them, a rich, full life is lived through a commitment to family and hard work. And beneath that surface, there were also, as there are in all people, many dichotomies. How could they go through so much pain and suffering and still be kind? How could they, in one moment, be so hard and tough and in the next moment, be such loving and caring fathers and grandfathers? It takes a special kind of person to create balance out of those contradictions.

Because Giuseppe was blind and my pappou was still taking care of our laundromats, I actually spent many of my summer days with Giuseppe. We would sit at my grandmother's kitchen table and play dominos. My grandmother would make a jug of iced tea, and we would play for hours. The dominos had raised dots, so Giuseppe could feel them with his hands. We played every day. The summer breeze would kick in from the open kitchen windows, and we would sit in our undershirts. We would sit and listen to Italian music.

He liked Caruso and playing dominos, and he talked a lot about construction. I remember he told me why streets are pitched higher in the middle—so when it rains, the water goes to the sides. He told me the Romans first thought of this. He would also talk about the Italian aqueducts. He was a great admirer of what the Romans accomplished with construction, and he carried that ancient tradition of quality construction within him.

Every holiday family members would play Spit, a very simple card game in which each player attempts to unload their deck of cards the fastest. It's essentially a game of speed that always turns into psychological warfare. My mother and I were always the best at it. It requires fast reactions, a trait that my mother, grandfather, and myself have more than anyone else. We think fast and we act fast. My mom and I would play Spit and the whole table would shake as we slammed the cards down. Trash talking often erupted, and Giuseppe loved that. He loved any kind of competition. He and pappou would have pancake-eating contests on Sundays when our family went to IHOP. I am told that when he was sighted, he was very athletic. My mom and I are both athletic as well.

One of my mom's favorite games is ping pong. When she was a teenager, my mother went on vacation with her family to Greene County in the Catskills to a place called Pleasant Farms. I know the place because I went there as well when I was a child. It's two hours north of New York City in an area where there are green mountains, chilly creeks and reminders of the Rip Van Winkle legends. Whenever we went there it was Sinatra music, the pool and games. It was our small getaway, and the whole family would go. When my mother was a child, all of her aunts, uncles and cousins would go as well.

Pleasant Farms is gone now, sold to the owner of a Jewish boys' camp, but in the old days, it had an overwhelmingly Italian environment. One of the funniest stories about the resort was about one big shot guy who was beating everyone in everything and bragging loudly about his prowess. One year this stereotypical figure was on a roll until it came to ping pong. Little did he know that the Vacca family had a ping pong table in their basement amidst neatly piled tools and other construction materials. My mother was a teenager at the time, but of course, she challenged him. The big shot was confidently talking, saying he would take it easy on my mother, asking her if she needed to warm up for the first few points. It took a couple volleys, and then my mom buried him. The tables turned and as she continued to win, she began to echo his questions back to him and add her own. Things like, "maybe you should stretch?" or "are you crying?" were added to the banter. Giuseppe was laughing so hard that he was the one in tears. He always enjoyed telling that story about my mother, who stands maybe 5'1".

My mother's small stature is actually in total juxtaposition to her gregarious personality and her undeniable power. When my mother enters a room, people notice. Although she's Italian, she can truly be described with the word *shpirto*. My pappou was very close to her, and they immediately got along. I think it's because it is clear that she can express her own kind of *philotimo* but also can be resilient, like pappou's mother. That was how my grandfather, Giuseppe, always described her.

I'm much the same way. We are both like Giuseppe—very nice and kind until we aren't. My sister on the other hand has an infinite amount of patience. I'm trying to learn from her. I need to temper my tendency to expect the worst in people, and constantly have my guard up.

Giuseppe, like pappou, dressed sharply when he and I weren't sitting around his house wearing undershirts. It was dress slacks every day and starched button-down cotton shirts. The only times I saw him not wearing black slacks was when we went to the public pool together. We would also compete at the pool to see who could hold their breath for the longest. I wanted to win so badly that I fainted once because I stayed under water too long.

Giuseppe was incredibly disciplined. Even after he went blind, he was able to quit smoking. When my mother and his doctor explained to him how unhealthy smoking was, he quit within a couple of months. When he developed diabetes, he had to change his entire diet, and he did it immediately. He didn't cheat on his diet, and he didn't sneak cigarettes. I admired his self-discipline, and that is another thing I strive to embody from Giuseppe.

We also both liked yelling. When we went to the Jersey Shore with my mother, sister, and my grandma Elizabeth, Giuseppe and I would drive everyone nuts by singing (yelling, really) opera in the car. We both simply liked action and noise. Since we had to sit still in the car, we would blast opera over the radio and yell along with it.

He had a very rough exterior, but he was also sensitive, even artistic at times. He built a beautiful tray ceiling in my grandmother's living room that has different colored lights that switch on and off when you turn them on. It is a very large oval that takes up most of the ceiling. My grandmother always wanted clouds painted in that space above the chandelier, but Giuseppe went blind before he could finish it. Recently, when I started working and finally had some money, I found an artist who painted clouds for her. I was living the code, standing in for Giuseppe, and completing his vision even though he was gone. I got the job done.

I was thinking about the fact that Giuseppe was gone from our lives the next time I visited with pappou to hear more of his story. It was mid-November, and pappou was clearly weakening. He made no pretense of not using his cane, and he didn't stand up when I entered the room. There was a slight tremor in his right hand, and his voice was weaker, sometimes so hoarse I could barely hear him. But his eyes were the same—sparkling, clear blue, steady on me, looking to see my reaction, I never let on that I was noticing that he was getting weaker; to do so would've been to rob him of his dignity. He knew that I knew he was not doing well, but we also agreed, by glances and shrugs, not to talk about it. I recalled that I never heard Giuseppe say the word blind. We would spend hours, days and weeks together, and I never heard that word.

I also thought about Giuseppe when yiayia brought out a pitcher of iced tea to drink while we listened to pappou. It was an unusually warm fall afternoon. The windows were open and the breeze from outside ruffled the curtains. For just the briefest of moments, I wanted to reach for a set of dominos and pretend that we were all playing together, that I was just a kid again, that it was eternal summer, not temporary fall, that life was frozen in time and Giuseppe was alive and pappou was not dying.

Yiayia asked me how my thesis was coming along, and I told her the writing was going well, but I was eager to listen to another story if pappou felt up to it. "Oh yes," she said, "he looks forward to your visits. We miss you so much, Bill." She was calling me by my father's name again. Time stopped. The pleasant breeze wafting through the open windows seemed to grow still. Pappou glanced up slowly. Yiayia placed two fingers across her lips. "I mean…Perry," she said. The moment passed.

I was about to ask pappou if he wanted to remain on the couch, but then I saw him lean into his cane with both hands and push himself up. He was determined that there would be no changes in our routine.

Pappou swayed briefly, but both yiayia and I sensed that reaching out to steady him would only embarrass him. He righted himself and slowly shuffled to the table. He stood erect, chin up, his head held high.

Then he sat down. We took our places, and the familiar ritual began.

* * *

The Sixth Story:

The Pavlou Mela concentration camp was the main prison that the occupying forces, the Germans, Italians and Bulgarians, had established just outside the city of Thessaloniki, Greece. While many horrors, torture and executions took place in the camp, it was better known as the Greek transit point for the deportation of prisoners to Auschwitz and Treblinka. So we knew when we arrived at Pavlou Mela that that it was just a rest stop before moving on to the Nazi slaughterhouses.

Outside the camp doors there were two sentinels with automatic weapons, and there were observation posts every ten meters. Once we were herded like sheep through the heavy iron doors, we were quickly whipped and pushed into another holding area. Then huge iron doors closed behind us again.

When the Germans captured us on a farm, we were carrying a pitchfork and a sickle because we were harvesting in the fields. When we entered those gates, we were called Andartes. The Nazis collected young people, women, and old people to send them to Germany where they were slaughtered, because the beast was enraged by its inability to conquer Greece, so they considered capturing the weak a success. Hitler sent six fully armed war divisions to exterminate women and children, to extinguish entire villages and cities. They captured unarmed civilians and presented them as rebels just for the so-called victory of creating thousands of corpses.

At Pavlou Mela, Panayiotis and I were held with about three hundred Serbians who had been captured in battle. Then we were taken to a barber, and he completely shaved both of our heads. We were shoved through a narrow hallway with all the others who were also getting shaved. We shuffled along silently. Then we were led into a room where we stripped naked and we then gave them our clothes to be cleaned. They had to wash our clothes three times to get rid of the lice. We showered, and then we were given ointment that we applied over our entire bodies. Once we dressed and went back outside, the

Serbians called us over and offered us food, but they did that in secret. We didn't take the food because we were afraid that if the Germans found out we had food, they would kill us.

We wanted to avoid getting the soldiers' attention at all costs. Our cousin was an Andarte, and we knew the Germans hated men like our cousin. If they discovered that our cousin was a captain of the rebels, we would have been killed on the spot. Any sort of victory, even killing two young farmers who had a rebel cousin, was welcomed.

Okay, so we were confined in the camp, and we needed to find a way to survive, and to send word to our family that we were alive. We discovered that a man named Militades Mouratides from Melanthio, another small village in Kastoria near our village, was in the camp. We also learned that he was leaving the camp. We knew him, so the day before he left, we asked him if he could deliver a message to our father. We asked him to please let our father know that we were alive and that we were still together. He agreed, and we hoped that he would be able to deliver it. But that was the only contact we could find with the outside world. We were totally confined to the dark, cold walls of the camp that was filled to the brim with hostages. We were all just numbers.

The Serbians were regular soldiers who were captured in fierce battles, so they were treated well by the Red Cross. They were allowed to receive packets of food and pastries and coffee and cigarettes. After we lost our fear that being friendly with them would make the Germans angry, my brother and I got close with this group, and they always shared whatever they had with us. The Serbians and the Greeks got along very well in the camp, and we helped each other survive. They would whistle to us and call us over to their section of the camp. They hid pastries in napkins and passed them to us as we walked by. We would thank them and walk away, unwrapping the treats and splitting them between us. Those were moments when we could forget where we were, if only for a second. Eating these pastries and candies reminded us of our father coming home from his trips. Moments like these kept us afloat.

Near the Serbian section was the part of the camp for the prisoners who had been sentenced to death. It was much larger than the Serbian part. It was also the execution and torture wing. People were taken at random in groups of twenty to thirty people, and they never came back. This was also the place where people were held until they were sent to another place to be killed. But sometimes they were killed at Pavlou Mela or died in their cells. These people had often been taken as reprisals of some sort. If there was a problem with the citizens in some town square, they would randomly select twenty people and place them in these death cells.

One day, an interpreter came and read names from a list of about 2,000 people. He ordered us to be ready early in the morning for departure to Germany, where we would work in the factories. This was what they constantly told us, that they were taking people to work, but in reality, they were taking them to be slaughtered. The same information was written in the newspapers. People who left for Germany or Poland never came back.

In the morning they started loading the trains. They were loading people into the freight cars all the way from the camp back to the railroad station. Everyone was squished together inside the cars like cattle. We heard that trains that were leaving for Germany frequently stopped along the way to remove people who died of asphyxiation. They stopped in the mountains and made the hostages bury the dead. This was done to prevent other nations from knowing about the size of their atrocities. Each day we watched as people poured in by the hundreds, and then every day they were cleared out and stuffed onto the trains. There were only eighty-five to one hundred of us that for some reason were kept at the army camp.

As the interpreter was announcing the names, everyone was grouped in front of him. They would all stare at him in the hope that their name would not be called.

We were standing in the crowd with the others when I noticed one man moving through the crowd. He was staring fiercely at the man announcing the names, and he was aggressively pushing through the crowd toward the front. Then he got past the front row of prisoners and lunged at the man announcing the names.

The armed guards that stood next to the interpreter were too slow and the fierce man pulled a homemade knife from his waist and stabbed the interpreter. As the wild man stabbed the interpreter, the guards immediately hit him with the butts of their guns. The whole crowd scattered in fear that the guards would open fire.

The interpreter fell to his knees and was bleeding badly from his stomach. I looked on from a distance and saw that the guards knocked the wild man unconscious and then they dragging his body away from the scene. Nurses soon arrived to help, and everyone was on edge for the next couple of days because we were waiting for the Germans to get their revenge on us for that man's act. As for him, he was never seen again.

Around this time, we also kept hearing about a man everyone referred to as "the barber." The rumor was that there was a man in a town near the camp who worked as a barber, but also for the Andartes. They said he was responsible for planting that man in our camp and that he was helping people escape. We didn't have enough information to find him but we both remembered "the barber" in case we were able to escape and make it to his village.

One day, the guards started talking to all the young men around our age, and they then started to separate us into different groups. Panayiotis and I were both sitting on the floor when we saw the officers coming toward us. We panicked because we thought the guards were looking for us because of our cousin.

When we saw that they were talking to every young man they passed, we were calmed for a moment. Then we realized that they were separating people by their age. We were both panicked and we did not know what to do. They reached the both of us and asked how old we were. I said I was 15 and Panayiotis said he was 16. The soldier grabbed me by the arm and pulled me away from my brother. I resisted.

The interpreter with the guards yelled at me to come. He said that I was being taken to another camp. A soldier tightened his grip on my arm, and Panayiotis and I both stood with shocked looks on our faces. There was no point in fighting unless we wanted to be killed.

I was taken and Panayiotis was left behind. We were separated, so we couldn't talk to each other. As usual, armed soldiers escorted us, but as we walked away, we exchanged a glance and a nod. We both knew that we wouldn't leave each other.

I was taken to a regular German army camp that was located near Pavlou Mela but outside the concentration camp. There, I was trained to be a German soldier. Every day, I was forced to dig roads and holes; we were taught to dig ditches in a zigzag pattern to prevent tanks from approaching the camp. We would do that every morning, and after we were done digging, we were taken to a gymnasium and trained by a German captain. Every day was the same, and every day was regimented.

I learned that I was in a camp where the Nazis prepared food for their army, and that they were training me to fight for them on the Eastern front. I later found out the Germans did this in all nations they occupied. They would find young men, train them to be German soldiers, and then send them to fight in a different area from where they were captured, usually to the front in Russia. I knew if I did not find a way to escape and return to my brother, I would be lost forever in a foreign country or killed in battle. I had no choice; I had to think of a way to escape.

***

When he stopped talking, pappou's voice was a mere whisper; I poured him a glass of iced tea. He smiled and took a sip. He rolled his tongue across his lips, drank some more. Yiayia commented, "He's very tired," she said.

Pappou waved his hand in front of us. "No, no, I'm okay."

I didn't want to push him to expend any more energy, but pappou seemed to want to sit and talk for a while. Because I had been thinking about Giuseppe, I said, "Remember the time you and Giuseppe were playing dominoes and he won twice in a row?"

Pappou smiled. "Never."

"He did. I was there."

Pappou shook his head in good-natured denial. "He may have beat me twice, but he never beat me twice *in a row*."

We were both quiet for a few moments, alone with our memories. Then pappou sighed. "Ah, Giuseppe, I miss him. He was a good, good friend, a brother."

"Did you ever talk about the war with him?"

"No, not really. You know, in Greece, the Italians weren't brutal, like the Germans."

"Anyway, pappou, he was already an American when the war came. He fought against the Nazis and was stationed in Germany."

"Yes Perrymou, I remember he told me a little about that. You know, here in New York, in the Bronx, Italians and Greeks, we are friends. The others, they treat us the same."

"The others?"

Yiayia interrupted. "You know what he means, Perry. Italians and Greeks … too loud, too hairy."

I laughed in spite of myself, because I thought about how I may look to some of my classmates at Columbia.

One of the reasons I went to Columbia was because when I was a kid we would often pass their football field located at the most northern tip of Manhattan when my father and pappou and me were running errands going to and from the Bronx and Inwood. We would be driving in my dad's beat up old car in dirty clothes, smelling like a mix of pizza dough and WD 40 among the other aromas that came with working in the pizzerias and working on the laundry machines. I would ride in the back while my father drove and pappou was riding shotgun. They would mostly be speaking Greek which I only half understood, and I would gaze out the window at the football field. I remember thinking to myself that I should go there—go to Columbia. I would actually pray that I could go there.

I forgot about that fantasy for about a decade, and then I ended up going to Columbia for my Master's Degree. As I sat there in my classes, I knew I still smelled like pizzerias and laundromats, and that made me even more proud to be there. From counting quarters to Columbia.

"Yeah, yiayia," I said, "I know what he means."

The sunlight was beginning to fade, and the warm breeze that had been so pleasant turned chilly. The warm weather was leaving and soon it would be winter. Yiayia left the table and went over to close the window. She stayed standing next to the curtains for some time, staring out at the street, watching intently, something... or nothing. Then she turned abruptly. "Do you want to eat, Perry?"

I shook my head, no.

"You should eat. You're too thin. You don't look so good."

When I was little, I was a chubby kid. At Giuseppe's house my grandmother Elizabeth would make macaroni and meatballs every day, and chocolate cake. Every day: macaroni, meatballs and chocolate cake. I always ate the cake on a *mappin*, that's Italian-American slang for a towel. I would lie on my stomach facing the television and go to town on the rich food. Watching *The Price Is Right* and playing card games were also staples of our routine.

Food is both the solution and the problem in my family. If you're thin, they make you eat, and then if you're overweight you become material for jokes. There's no winning at this game. Just a week before this discussion, my father, who had recently put on a few pounds, was at the house helping pappou with some bookkeeping. I was sitting with yiayia on the couch and she turned to me.

"Watch this."

I looked at her with a slight smile. "Ok." I replied.

She turned her head towards my father and pappou and said,

"Billy, you look like you've lost some weight."

My father, with a bright, smiling reaction said, "Thanks, ma."

She turned back to me, puffed air into her cheeks mocking him and as she was laughing and said, "He believed me."

I told my father about this in the car ride home and he jokingly blamed her for his portliness. He cited a barbeque in the early 1970s when his weight began to grow along with yiayia's suggestions that he eat more. A few ribs later, and his meteoric rise to shopping in the husky boy section began. This short memory brought a smile to my face as I once again declined yiayia's suggestion to eat with them.

Pappou stood and leaned on his cane. "Leave the boy alone, yiayia. He looks good, fit and trim. Like a fighter. Hungry." He made his way back to the couch. "He works hard."

"Thanks, pappou."

Pappou reached for the remote control and turned on the TV. The Greek channel. He was done talking for the day. Yiayia walked away from the window and sat down on the couch next to my grandfather. Take away all those years and they were like a young couple on their first date.

I let myself out, headed for home. Giuseppe was still on my mind. When I reached my room, I popped in an old Luciano Pavarotti CD of Puccini's *Turandot* and turned up the volume. My mother came into my room and said: "That's the CD we played in the car when we went to the beach with grandpa."

"Yea," I said as the extremely emotional aria *Nessun Dorma* ("Nobody Shall Sleep") began. *Nessun Dorma* is sung by the unknown prince when he challenges his love—the cold princess Turnadot—to discover his real name before dawn. If she does, she may execute him and if she does not, she must marry him. As the aria developed, I began to sing, yelling as loud as possible, as Giuseppe and I used to do. I looked at my mother and there were tears streaming down her cheeks. Then she too began to sing with me until we reached my favorite line *"all' alba vincerò,"* ("at dawn I will win"), and then we both stopped singing and let the power of Pavarotti's voice carry us through to the final line: "Vincerò! Vincerò!" ("I will win! I will win!").

I wrapped my arms around my mother with a smile on my face. For a few painfully brief but beautiful moments, I clearly remembered those summer days with Giuseppe. As the song played, I thought about the significance of the lines that ring out. They were like a declaration of a brazen mentality and an affirmation of life. If we're lucky enough to wake up, we should try our best to be good at all that we do. And we will win.

CHAPTER 7

Dancing in the Dark

"Love interprets between gods and men [humans], conveying and taking across to the gods the prayers and sacrifices of men, and to men the commands and replies of the gods... For God mingles not with man; but through Love,"

—**Diotima of Mantinia**,
priestess and philosopher who plays an important role in Plato's Symposium.

Pappou was very respectful toward yiayia, and he saw her as a full partner in their lives together. Although he held a very traditional view of what it means to be a man—strength, power, hard work and providing for his family, "he also felt, thought, and embodied the idea that women were strong, powerful, and hard-working, and played equal roles in providing for a family. He and yiayia shared everything in their lives and they both maintained their equal partnership into old age.

In the 1950s, it was not uncommon in the Greek-American community that marriages would be arranged by family members or friends. Matchmaking was an art form that was bestowed upon certain members of the community who seemed to have a special talent for bringing people together. This was the case with a woman named Didi, who was a mutual friend of both my grandparents and was responsible for introducing them.

At that time (and to some degree, even today) when Greeks determined they wanted to marry other Greeks, it was not unusual for people to search for a significant other who was from their same region in Greece. Yiayia's parents were both from Kastoria, as was pappou. The social circles were very tight, and they were maintained by matchmakers who had the same mentality.

Pappou was always exceedingly charming, and yiayia was a kind-hearted but stern woman. When I was young, she was very sharp, very clever. Whenever she played checkers with us, she would win. I also remember she would read the newspaper every morning, as well as a collection of magazines. She was constantly cutting out articles that she thought were relevant for someone in the family. I liked sports when I was young, so she cut out sports articles for me. She would call people and read parts of articles to them that she thought would help them in some way. I have many memories of articles cut from this newspaper or that magazine being shared at our dining room table. Like pappou, she was unexpectedly worldly because of her reading habits. She was also very fashionable. There's a photo that my sister particularly likes of yiayia wearing Ray Bans, looking like a poet or hipster.

When she was a child, yiayia loved to dance, and she wanted to be a dancer. Of course, that was not a suitable career for a Greek-American woman in the years when she was growing up, so her mother forbid her to even think about being a dancer. She would tell stories about how she loved gym in school and was very active.

I have fond memories from photos of her dancing in costume at Greek festivals, and even randomly dancing around her house. It was not until recently that I finally gained an understanding of what it means when Greeks raise their arms while dancing the *Zebekiko*. I have such vivid memories of yiayia walking around the house and all the sudden hitting that pose as the music came on, but I never knew that is symbolizes the eagle's wings and freedom from the shackles of despair by taking flight. Yiayia was always there to lift us up.

I also don't agree with the notion of a gender hierarchy. As Camus said, "Don't walk behind me, I may not lead. Don't walk in front of me; I may not follow. Just walk beside me and be my friend." That is how I have always understood the relationships between the men and women in my family. At times, my father leads, and at other times, my mother leads. The bottom line is that everything is done together for each other.

I can't see any kind of strict or rigid gender hierarchy, since I have always known women like yiayia, my grandmother, Elizabeth, and my mother, who is a combination of Xena, the fictional Warrior Princess, and Maria Montessori, the renowned innovator in early childhood educational theories. These powerful women, along with my sister, informed my understanding of the extraordinary capabilities of women.

I really do respect the power that anyone can wield. If I have daughters and sons, both sexes will play sports, appreciate art and play instruments. I like to see gender issues through the perspective of the ancient Spartan notion of having men and women train together. Power and strength are for everyone and men who don't understand that are simply weak.

Pappou told me that when he first came to America, he wrote letters to his mother back in Greece asking for advice. That sort of relationship is very similar to the relationship I have with my mother. She is my *consigliere,* and I often look to her for her opinions on all of the most important decisions I make. I have always been, and still can be, very open with my mother about the details of my life. I am an open person in general, but I do not often ask people outside of my parents for advice on difficult topics.

The stereotype that mothers have a special place in Italian and Greek culture is true, at least it was true in my family. Their opinions really matter and their feelings and well-being are of the utmost importance. There's an interesting set of priorities when it comes to how one treats their mother. You could be a lawyer, or a criminal, and either way, if you don't take care of your mother, you're considered a failure. Even when a person's life has been marred by bad decisions, if he takes his mother out on Sundays, people find a way to highlight that he isn't all that bad. In the same way that my father told me I'm less important than my sister, he would also admit that he is less important than my mother. I know that may seem like a strange comment, but to be a member of the family is to put other people before yourself and that is especially true for moms and sisters.

When I reflect on the core of my strong relationship with my mother, I reach the conclusion that it comes from my ability to share things with her that I have a tendency to censor when I'm talking with others. I know I can tell her exactly what I think and feel about anything because that sort of frankness and openness is how she raised us to interact with her. Her motto is: tell me everything and never lie to me because a lie is an insult. She would rather know everything and then help me, or tell me that I'm an idiot, so we can move on. We really hate liars in my family, and my mother, especially, is a realist, so she likes to have all the facts.

If I have characterized both my grandfathers and myself as having pride in work that borders on being obsessive, then I must include my mother in that description. She is an education professor, and she is phenomenal. I remember, as a child, watching her work to get her PhD while raising two children and running the household. I still marvel at her intensity today when it comes to her career—it isn't just a job; her work is a part of who she is. We don't believe in a work/life balance, we believe in a work/life synergy. I think that synergy is one of the reasons she is such a great mother, wife, friend and teacher.

I've seen her teach, and watching her is truly inspiring. If a person who didn't speak English sat in on one of my mother's classes, they would still be able to feel that she is a great teacher. The ability to attract and connect with people that my pappou, Giuseppe, and I have, she has as well. She runs a classroom in exactly the same way her father, Giuseppe, ran a construction site—with confidence, intensity and high standards.

Watching her teach or hearing Giuseppe talk about his work was like watching a prizefight. We don't have a problem telling people we're good. We know our strengths and our weaknesses. If you asked any of us, "Are you good at basketball?" we would have no problem saying no. But if you asked Giuseppe, "Hey Joe, can you lay concrete?" He would say, "I'm the best." If someone asked my mom, "Hey Lisa, can you teach education courses?" She would say, "Better than anyone." Of course, she would be correct, unless I'm in the room to argue with her about it and stake my claim. This is mostly just a fun way we all compete and assert ourselves. Really, it is also a motivator to keep us growing and trying. As Heraclitus said, "big results require big ambition." Saying you're the best teacher in a room full of teachers to us is a statement of purpose more than an assertion of how things are. If we show up, we are going to try to be the best.

My mother's deep and profound passion and confidence in her work is something that makes her who she is. Her approach to her work is also something that she had to fight for. Giuseppe went blind when she was only 16 and still attending a local high school in the Bronx. When she began working more, going to school became so difficult that she almost dropped out. She decided to finish high school and completed her undergraduate work. After college, she started her Master's at Fordham University in teaching.

After her Master's she turned to my father, who she had recently married and asked if he thought she should join a gym or go to graduate school for her doctorate. He suggested school and she started her doctorate at Fordham University the next semester in Language, Literacy and Learning. She excelled in the doctoral program, graduating when she was 34 years old. She spent the early years of her career teaching students at a variety of grade levels. Then she worked at an institution that serves teenaged boys with emotional disabilities. After that she became a professor at Manhattan College where she would become the Chair of the Education Department years later. She can teach anyone.

Not everything is so serious between us. We joke around a lot, and we often work together. We are both educators, so if you visit our house, you will find us at the kitchen table surrounded by books. She was the person who inspired me, along with other professors from Manhattan College like Dr. David Bollert who wrote a recommendation letter on my behalf for graduate school. Now that I am an adjunct professor at Manhattan College, the three of us will often sit and talk in my mother's office. I've often had moments observing the both of them talk as I sit in the room, and it truly occurs to me how I lucky I am to have the both of them as mentors and colleagues. My mother is passionate about being a professor, and I also developed that mentality.

My sister, Christina, is another smart, caring woman and a teacher as well. We are only a couple of years apart, and we have always been very close. When we were growing up, it was always important that we took care of each other. The phrases "watch out for your sister," or "watch out for your brother," were a constant admonition from my parents.

She is infinitely calmer than I am, and therefore more laid back. She is generally very easy-going, and we often ask each other for opposite kinds of advice. I encourage her to take action and get motivated, and she often encourages me to calm down. I usually start with "Am I being crazy?" and she usually starts with "How can I do this?" She is someone who I would genuinely like even if she wasn't my sister. She is more similar in temperament to my father, and I am more similar to my mother. Where I am usually loud and intense, she is calm and quiet.

Christina is also less impulsive than I am. We recently had a conversation on her birthday about how she plans to live the rest of her life within ten minutes of where we currently live. And, she is following a career path that she discovered in her early childhood, which is something I envy because I have already changed careers three times. She is the stable voice of reason that I turn to for council when my own journey gets a little off kilter.

It is because I have these experiences with strong women, and experiences of how women in my family handle themselves, that I began to find it difficult to see yiayia when I came by the house to hear pappou's stories. Yiayia was still physically strong and agile, but it was becoming increasingly clear that her mind was failing and her concentration wandered.

It was another unusually warm day in late November the last time I could visit and still meet pappou in his garden. Yiayia answered the door, and I could tell that at first she wasn't certain who I was. I gave her a big smile anyway and said, "It's Perry, yiayia." I kissed her, which pleased her. Then I asked, "Is pappou waiting for me in the living room?"

Yiayia frowned. "No, he's…" And then she went silent.

"Is he in his bedroom?"

She stared at me. Then she said, "Pappou is in the garden."

I found him huddled on his usual bench with a heavy sweater wrapped tightly around his shoulders that seemed thinner each time I saw him. His cane was next to him. The fruit trees had lost their leaves, and the tomato plants were mostly all withered and brown. The sun was low in the sky, and a brisk wind blew the fallen leaves up against the fence at the edge of the garden.

I knelt down in front of him and held his hands in mine; they were cold.

"Pappou, let's go inside," I suggested.

We slowly made our way into the house. He leaned on my left arm and held his cane firmly in his right hand until we reached our regular place at the table. Yiayia wandered into the room and took her regular place next to me.

At first, I wasn't sure we were going to proceed. Yiayia and I both waited for pappou to catch his breath. Then he sat upright. He opened the notebook and read a few lines to himself. Then he raised his head and looked at me. His eyes were clear, and he began to speak.

***

The Seventh Story:

After the collapse of the German forces at the invasion of Normandy, France, in the summer of 1944, anyone could see the Germans were going to lose the war. When I received this news, I rejoiced because I thought the end was near, but Hitler refused to accept defeat. Instead, he began extinguishing everyone and everything. It was crazy because there was no chance of winning once the Americans had joined in, and the German army was losing ground every day. So these new deaths were only death for death's sake. I knew that I had to get my brother out of Pavlou Mela, and that we had to escape.

However, before I could act, bombs from the British air force hammered Thessaloniki. They were dropping bombs all around us, because the British were aiming for the German camps. One night, when the alarm went off and the bombs began to fall, I ran to find shelter in the camp. The entire region was shaking from the explosions. All the trains, artillery, and vehicles were shattered to pieces. When I left the shelter, it seemed like everything was erased. Our camp was destroyed, and I got word that Pavlou Mela was also hit very hard by the bombings. There was no one to stop me, so I went to visit Panayiotis after the bombings to make sure he was still alive.

As I walked through the gates of Pavlou Mela, it looked like a ghost town. There were no more hostages arriving at the depot and all the buildings and storage areas seemed empty. My stomach dropped, and I thought the worst had happened. There were only a few hostages left, and only a handful of officers walking around.

I went up to one of the hostages and asked him what happened. He told me that after the bombing, the Nazis had taken more people than ever on the remaining trains to Germany. I frantically asked that person if he had seen my brother. I gave the hostage my brother's name and described him. The hostage said no, he hadn't seen anyone that fit that description.

I felt the air being sucked out of my lungs, each breath was getting heavier. What if they had put him on the trains? I ran to the first officer I could find and tried to ask him what was going on. I told him about my brother and again I described him. The officer said that almost all of the Greeks had been taken away on the trains. I was heartbroken. I thought I had failed him, but I refused to give up and kept looking around the camp.

As I was looking, an old woman approached me and asked me what I was doing. I told her that I was looking for my brother. When I described Panayiotis she said there was a young Greek boy who was sent to the infirmary with a horrible fever. I asked her where the infirmary was, and she gave me directions. I ran as fast as I could and opened the door to the infirmary to find my brother, pale as a ghost sitting, in a bed all by himself. The fever had saved his life. I grabbed his hand and kissed his forehead. He was barely able to speak from the fever. I knew I had to find a way to get him out before they sent the last of the Greeks away on the trains. I told him that we were going to get out of there. I left him that day with a heavy heart, but I had a goal in mind.

Since I was then, technically, a German soldier, I had access to the German officers. Once I knew I had to get my brother out of Pavlou Mela, I decided that I would speak to the general at my camp. I walked into his office and he was standing there with his arms at his sides. He was meticulously dressed, with his bright, yellow hair parted to the side. I was wearing my soldier's uniform, so after I gave the tyrant's salute, I began speaking to the general in a calm tone. I told him that my brother was in the Pavlou Mela and that he was very sick. I told him that I was worried about Panayiotis, and I would like to get him out of Pavlou Mela. He stared at me with a blank gaze and then said, "I only worry because I did not capture your brother sooner." I stared back at him, blank, angry, and stunned. The war was over and I knew that he knew this was true. There was no point in keeping us any longer—the dogs had heeled. I saluted, turned, and walked out of his office.

I was shaking with anger, as I walked down the stairs. I clenched the banister and tears began to run down my face. After taking a few steps, I heard the general's clerk yell to me, "Come back! The general wishes to speak with you."

I collected myself and walked back up the stairs and back into the room. The general was standing with his hands folded in front of him and said, "Don't worry. Give all the credentials to the secretary, your brother's name, and surname." I exhaled, looked up at him, thanked him, saluted, and left his office for the final time.

When I went back to Pavlou Mela, my brother was dressed in a military uniform. He began to tell me about what he had experienced. They were going to load him onto a train for Germany when his fever hit, and he couldn't move. I looked at him after he finished telling me about his time spent in the infirmary, and I said that it was unbelievable that he was still alive. I told him again that we needed to get out of there.

We made a plan to escape. There was a group of men I had met who wanted to go with us. Panayiotis and I went back to my camp, and I rounded them up. We decided we would risk everything with these men. We knew if we were caught trying to escape, we would be killed, but we all shared the same courage and the same fear. We took an oath to keep our plan a secret. If the worst happened and one of us was caught, we pledged to never give up the others. We all shook hands and went our separate ways. My brother returned to his company, and I went to mine.

Within days, one of the men we planned to escape with overheard officers talking outside the barracks, and we discovered that the Germans were planning on sending us to fight in Russia. I knew then that we had made the right decision to escape and that we had to do it soon. We had to find a way to get out of Thessaloniki as soon as possible. I remembered rumors about the man the others called "the barber." I asked a few Greeks in the camp and they told me where to find him. I went and found my brother. We gathered everyone together and we told them that we would go that afternoon.

We never knew this "barber's" name, but we soon learned that he worked with the underground resistance and the Andartes, and that he was smuggling people out of the camps. We approached him and asked about how we could get out. He calmly looked at us and said, "You must take all your belongings without leaving anything behind. This includes clothes, blankets, and boots, everything you have. The day after tomorrow, at 7:00 pm, all of you will come here to my barber shop."

We made the arrangements to get leave from our camps, and we all met together on time at the place where the barber told us we should be. We waited a few moments in silence. When the barber got there, he took us to a hidden shelter. This was where we would stay until the moment was right and we could make our escape.

The barber seemed like he had experience with this routine, and we trusted him. He moved with a calm anger. He didn't say much—only what needed to be said, and his eyes always squinted whenever he spoke. He was about my height and always wore a hat. He was thin, like all of us who had been affected by hunger. When he dropped us off at the shelter, all he did was stand in front of us, nod, and then turn and walk away as the door closed behind him.

At around 1:00 am the next morning, the alarm began wailing, warning that the English bomber planes were returning. The crowds from the neighborhood gathered inside the shelter, but when two ladies came in, they stopped short when they saw us. They shouted, "Germans!"

The shock and terror on the women's' faces was unbelievable. They must have thought they had all been discovered. One of the men with us shouted, "No! No! We are Greeks!" He was from the women's village, and the barber, who had joined us again for the night, explained to everyone that we were Greeks dressed in German uniforms.

After about an hour, when the alarms quieted down, the Andartes brought in another person—a Frenchman. He worked in the offices of the military division, where he was a trusted clerk, and he spoke many languages, including Greek. Since he was a friendly man, we all exchanged our stories to pass the time.

Finally the day dawned, and at 10:00 am we asked the barber what was going on because we were obligated to make our appearance at our military camps soon. With his squinted eyes, he told us not to rush and that we would be leaving soon. We all continued to sit, wait, and talk. The Frenchman confirmed that we would have been sent to Russia to fight if we had not decided to escape. All of the others with us had stories similar to ours. They had also been captured while farming, or walking along the roads from village to village in order to trade goods; all of them were unarmed when they were taken prisoner.

That morning of October 6th, around 10:30, the barber said that it was time for us to leave Thessaloniki. I looked at the barber with a puzzled expression, "Now? It's broad daylight."

He smiled back at me, "Look at yourselves. You and your brother are dressed in the uniforms of German soldiers. Leave everything behind; it will look like you are just walking. No one will approach the group if they see that you and your brother are soldiers. If you are stopped, you will speak to the soldiers and tell them that you are escorting the rest of the group to a different prison camp. Let's hope they believe you."

So, the success of the escape rested on our shoulders. My brother and I exchanged glances and in a few moments we were walking out of the shelter. Two of the young Andartes joined us and we all walked down the road. My brother went to the front of the group, and I stayed in the back so that we would look more like an escort.

Each step felt heavy. We began by walking through the town. As we moved through the streets, we were all very nervous. My eyes were bouncing all over the place, but we made it outside the town and headed for Mount Chortiatis in the Asvestochori region. In the distance we saw a group of about twenty-five men holding what we thought were weapons so we stopped and talked amongst ourselves. We decided that if these men were Germans, Panayiotis and I would say that we were headed for a nearby village that we knew was under Nazi control.

One of the older guys decided that he would go ahead of the group to see if the men really were armed. He showed us two signals that he would make with his hands to let us know if it was safe or not. We moved forward slowly for half an hour and he signaled us, as he said he would, that it was safe. We climbed the mountain and saw that, in fact, these people were carrying pitchforks and other farming tools.

We kept moving forward. Right across from us, on the tip of Mount Chortiatis, the Germans had stockpiled a lot of equipment. They started blowing whistles and sirens went off. We were walking right across from the Germans. The mountain was bare, we had no cover; there was not a single shrub to hide us. If they used a machine gun, they would have completely cleared us out.

The two of us were still in uniform, and the others were dressed like civilians. We walked slowly, right in front of the German hillside. Everyone kept their eyes looking forward. I started counting my steps to stay focused. We walked and made it past. Again, we gazed at the viper and survived. We made it across the face of the mountain quickly, but each step felt like an eternity.

After we made it past Mt. Chortiatis, one of the young Andartes who had travelled with us turned and said, "Now you are free. You must walk quickly until you reach the ravine, at which point you will go to a small house, a safe haven. No German has ever set foot there."

We were reborn and out of the beast's clutches. We walked to the little house, and within hours of resting, more men arrived. They carried all of our belongings with them.

We finally felt safe; we were finally free. We all sat down outside the house and one of the men came up with a violin. He began to play, and I could feel the wheat in my hands, and for a moment, I could hear my mother singing. We all sang.

***

As he ended the story, pappou had a smile on his face. For once, the narrative ended on a happy note, and that feeling seemed to give him strength. He closed the notebook and pressed his palms against the table in order to stand up. "*Thelis pagoto*?" he asked.

This was a Greek phrase I was very familiar with because both pappou and yiayia loved ice cream.

"I would like some ice cream," said yiayia.

Pappou pushed his chair back and maneuvered toward the fridge. I stood and went with him, but I let him open the freezer himself and take out the ice cream while I found three bowls. He turned to me and with a sly grin said, "Perrymou, you can scoop." We both knew he could not.

Minutes later we were all three sitting at the table eating ice cream. There was no escaping without his brother, and there was no eating ice cream without yiayia.

"Your mother had to be so happy to see you and Panayiotis," I said.

Pappou tilted his head quizzically. Then he understood what I meant. "Όχι ('no')," he said slowly. "We weren't home yet, Perry. We still had a long way to go before we were home." He sighed and slowly nodded his head up and down, remembering those first days away from the prison camps. "We were free, but not home."

I finished my ice cream, and set the bowl down. "It must have felt terrible wearing a German uniform."

Again, he stared off into the middle distance. "I was always Greek. I was never German. Wearing the uniform gave me my freedom. I would have never fought for them. Never."

"He hated them," said yiayia, as she surprised me with a such an astute contribution to the conversation. I turned toward her. She was lifting another spoonful of vanilla toward her lips. Her eyes were clear and sparkling like a young child's as she spooned the ice cream into her mouth. It made me so happy to see her like that.

"I hated them, but I needed to use them," said pappou. "If I had defied them, they would have killed me. They would have killed Panayiotis. Even the

Andartes understood. Once we were free and I changed into civilian clothes, they took my German uniform so others could put it to good use."

"It was like a costume," I said.

"Like a Halloween costume," said yiayia. She giggled.

Pappou even laughed. "'Ημουν ένα τέρας," he said, "I was pretending to be a monster to get my candy."

We were all three laughing and enjoying our ice cream. For that little while, it was like old times again.

I took our empty bowls to the sink, and then I packed my books and notes in order to leave. I kissed them both, and as I left, I heard the sounds of Greek television in the background. Another comedy. I hoped it would keep them laughing. Keep them happy.

Out on the street, a cold wind blew against my face. Winter was definitely coming. I was parked a few blocks away and had a couple minutes to reflect before reaching the warmth of my car. *He had to wear the swastika to free himself from the swastika.* His problem became his solution.

As I walked to my car with a copy of *The Plague* in my bag, wearing my black bomber jacket with a pen resting on my ear, I let my mind drift to thoughts of Camus and Seneca. *We have to acknowledge our pain to ever be free.* Just as Dr. Rieux, the main character in Camus' work, has to look at a dead rat and be the first to say there is a plague in the city in order for them to fight the sickness. We can train ourselves to step into our fears as a way of controlling them. If we can walk with our fears and not allow them to trouble us, we have conquered them.

Pappou and Giuseppe took advantage of this idea and made their freedom and chose to become the men they were and to live meaningfully. The universe turned to pappou and said, "Here, Sisyphus, push this rock, train as a soldier, wear our uniform." He made his own meaning and created the opportunity, brilliant. He said, "I was always a Greek," but he wore the mask of a Nazi, the uniform, to escape from them. The source of the pain gave him the freedom from the pain, absolute absurdity. Our courage to choose to live meaningfully in the face of the absurd conditions we find ourselves in is what we need.

I reached the door to the backseat and immediately started tearing through my bag. I grabbed a printed copy of the *Myth of Sisyphus* and in moments found the quote I was looking for. "…a blind man eager to see who knows that the night has no end, he is still on the go. The rock is still rolling."

I read those lines in my head, but more so in tribute to Giuseppe. He was also pushing the rock up the mountain with a smile, knowing that he would never see, but choosing to have a positive vision of life anyway.

Blindness comes from searching for meaning when we should be making it. Blindness comes from looking for the order and fairness that may not be there, from trying to discover it, rather than making it. We are not wanderers lost in a forest, we are my grandfather laying concrete, building.

My thoughts quieted for a moment as I closed the back door and opened the driver's side door. As I put the key into the ignition, I somehow knew it was the last time we would laugh together eating ice cream like we had just moments earlier. I didn't want to dwell on that thought, so I put my foot on the gas pedal and drove away.

CHAPTER 8

A Faint Flash of Red

"Don't explain your philosophy. Embody it."

—**Epictetus,**

Greek/Roman Stoic philosopher.

As the shorter winter days arrived and my pappou grew weaker, I sought out other members of my extended family in order to push deeper toward the taproot of my identity. To this day, I'm not entirely clear why this yearning to understand who I am took such a powerful hold on my consciousness during those bleak days. I suppose I was afraid that my grandfather's death would leave me feeling disconnected from my incredibly rich Greek heritage just at the time I was beginning to appreciate how powerful a hold my history had on me.

Although I was still struggling with my pappou's very Greek concept of *philotimo*, I was surprised to find that it was my Italian cousin, Frank, that I turned to.

I had heard stories about Frank from the days when he was working with my grandfather Giuseppe, about their constant arguments and their life-long friendship. Every day after they worked together, Frank would stop at Giuseppe's house and this inevitably would lead to some sort of disagreement that would escalate into yelling, but then Frank would show up the next morning to go to work, and then the very next evening they would go at it again. Frank still frequently calls my grandmother to make sure she's okay. Frank, to put it simply, is just as real and authentic as Giuseppe was, and therefore the person who provides the closest feeling to having my grandfather around that I could imagine. But before I started to hang out with him, he was more of a myth than an actual person.

One day I decided to call him and ask if he would mind sitting with me for a couple of hours to talk about Giuseppe and pappou. The ensuing conversation went from "a couple of hours" to an entire morning—a routine that was repeated over many Sundays.

Frank is a fit, intense man who resembles Robert DeNiro. He talks like DeNiro as well—the same short bursts of words spoken directly. He met me at the door, and before we went to sit down, he introduced me to his dogs. He is very proud of his pair of well-trained but very no-nonsense German Shepherds. He's always had German Shepherds. They are part of his persona. Apparently a gardener from his neighbor's yard almost got his arm ripped off because, as Frank put it, "he encroached."

As you can imagine, when we began talking, we disagreed immediately about politics and the economy and almost everything else. We argued. We fought. He would raise his eyebrows, put air into his upper lip and as he strongly hit the table with his fist, blurt out, "You believe that?" followed by "No, no, that's no good." That was usually in regard to any opinion I had that wasn't his, which included most of my opinions. Then we would talk some more.

Frank would spend hours explaining how the construction trade was passed down from my mother's family in Italy to Giuseppe in the Bronx, and then how Frank has grown the family business and passed it on to his son. The more we talked, the more I liked him.

One chilly Sunday morning after I'd stopped by his house in northern Westchester County, we sat, as usual, around the kitchen table and argued through endless cups of strong Italian coffee about the mayor of New York and conditions in the city, both topics about which we strongly disagreed. I liked the city. He didn't. To change the subject, I asked him if he thought my pappou had *philotimo*. "Phi…what?" he hunched his shoulders and held his hands in the air.

As I fumbled to explain the term, he interrupted me. "Okay, Perry, I get it. This *philotimo* thing reminds me of the Italian idea of *la bella figura*."

"The beautiful figure?"

"Yeah, but we're not talking Sophia Loren here, although she certainly did have *la bella figura*," he chuckled. "I'm talking about an Italian way of life that means if you're going to make an impression or a reputation, you should make a good one. You don't act like a fool in public, and you don't produce work that isn't your best because you always want to create *una bella figura*. In Italy, people don't leave the house looking like a mess and they don't keep a messy house." He stopped and looked directly at me. "You see my house?"

I laughed because we were sitting in his dining room. Frank loves to ask questions to which he knows the answers.

I replied "Yup."

His gaze was still locked as he responded with one word "Spotless."

He continued. "You don't want to dishonor your family or yourself by creating an ugly figure of yourself. You don't fight with your family in public and you don't talk trash about your family in public or to outsiders.

"You know, Perry, your grandfather Giuseppe and me, we weren't just 'in construction'. We cared about our buildings. We built beautiful buildings.

"In Italy, in Rome, there's a monument, the *Colosseo Quadroto*, the Square Coliseum, built during Mussolini's reign…" I wanted to interrupt him right there, but decided to let him go on. "On the building it says: *Un popolo di poeti, di artisti, di eroi, di santi, di pensatori, di scienziati, di navigatori, di trasmigratori;* a nation of poets, of artists, of heroes, of saints, of thinkers, of scientists, of navigators, of migrants. That's who we are, and we take pride in who we are. These are our values. If you don't stand by your values, you're a shmuck."

"But Mussolini…"

"I'm not talking about Mussolini, Perry. I'm talking about being Italian."

At the time, I'd been bouncing around between different part-time and full time jobs and when I asked for career advice he gave me the following: "Find something you like, but until then, you better get stupid and do whatever job you're doing the best you possibly can."

I chuckled at this advice that, from anyone else, I would have found offensive but I was reminded of a conversation I had with Marie, Frank's wife. Marie and Frank have been together for decades and they have three sons and two grandchildren. Marie is Sicilian and truly embodies the warmth of the Sicilian people. We were talking and she described what it was like growing up in East Harlem. She said, "You never had a problem, because everything was never only yours. Everybody was there for each other." That's how I feel when I turn to Frank and Marie for advice. I feel like I'm sitting with people who understand me and genuinely care, so nothing they say offends me.

With Frank, there are only two attitudes toward all things, right and wrong. I found this approach refreshing compared to the ambivalence I often faced at school. As Frank likes to say, "You walk with someone who has a limp, you're going to get a limp." Not a very politically correct way of putting it, but I get his point.

Talking to Frank is a form of baptism by fire, and some people can't handle it. Even Marie would often have to ask us to go outside because we were getting too loud. One of his son's girlfriends, after only knowing me for maybe twenty minutes turned to me at a dinner and said, "Your cousin Frank is really intense." My response was, "That's how we all are."

Whenever I talked to Frank, I would leave his house feeling proud and motivated. Although we disagree about so many things there is a real undercurrent of respect that we have for each other. He would never say this to me, but Marie told my mom that Frank really enjoyed our time together and he always asks about me when he calls my house and speaks to my mom. Frank is direct, authentic, and powerful. And those were qualities I especially admired and perhaps needed to be around as I watched my pappou fade.

The next time I visited pappou, my aunt was at his house. As life became more difficult for pappou, yiayia was overwhelmed taking care of him since her own problems weren't getting any better. For this reason, different members of the family were spending more and more time with pappou and yiayia, doing all the little things my grandparents either couldn't do or forgot to do.

My aunt spoke quietly, "It's good to see you, Perry." There were dark circles around her eyes, and her lips were drawn tightly. "He's on the couch waiting for you."

"How is he today?" I asked.

"He's..." she hesitated. "Anyway, he's been asking for you all morning."

"That's good."

She walked with me toward the living room. "These talks with you keep him going."

For the first time pappou didn't stand up when I entered the room, but he did have a smile on his face when he saw me. "Perrymou," he said softly. Yiayia was sitting next to him on the couch. She was also smiling.

My aunt suggested we might want to stay on the couch rather than moving to our usual place at the table. I glanced at pappou. He nodded in agreement, so I pulled up a chair and sat across from my grandmother and grandfather.

When I had a chance to really look at him, I was shocked by how much he had changed since I last saw him only a few days earlier. His eyes were sunken. His skin was sallow. He grimaced from time to time and I could tell he was in pain. His head leaned forward and his shoulders were hunched up toward his skinny neck.

I noticed there was a heating pad on the couch next to him. I reached out and put my hand on his shoulder, and I could feel his collarbone, sharp and protruding beneath his shirt. He clinched onto my hand and gripped tightly for a moment, then he sat back, patted his legs and said, "Let's go."

I asked if he and yiayia wanted to snack on something. They both said no. So, I realized there wouldn't be any more nuts or fruit or ice cream.

I sighed, lifted my bag off my shoulder and placed the notebook in his lap. He looked up briefly with a strained smile, looked down at the book and immediately, in a remarkable transition, his eyes cleared and his voice grew stronger.

***

The Eighth Story:

After we had gained our freedom in late August of 1944, Panayiotis and I were resting in the courtyard of that small house near Mt. Chortiatis, when we noticed a small, armed group of men sitting near us talking with each other, and it was clear from what they were saying that they were Andartes. My brother approached them and explained that some members of our group were from Kastoria and others were from the nearby village of Kozani, and we needed to return home to our families who had not seen us in months. "Our parents do not know where we are or whether we are dead or alive. What should we do?" asked Panayiotis.

The man turned to both of us and said "You are Andartes now. You will be going to our camp hidden in the mountains of northern Macedonia where you will be trained and take up arms." My brother suggested that we would prefer to go back to our hometown and take up arms there. I stood beside him during this conversation and nodded at Panayiotis' suggestion. The Andarte responded by saying, "We will be going to the camp and you will get settled there. You will be with the military division." We could see the sun setting in the window behind him. He ordered that we all move out of the house and begin marching toward their camp in the northern mountains. As it turned out, we weren't entirely free after all.

As we walked, we saw a large snake dash out across our path into a bush. I couldn't help but remember our capture. The French clerk who had been with us since we left Pavlou Mela nearly stepped on it. He turned to us and said, "It was a frog."

But I saw it pass right by him, and it was a snake.

One of the Andartes said, "That's a bad sign. Meeting a snake at sunset means death."

We kept walking, and as darkness fell, we stopped suddenly. One of the rebels turned sharply and said to listen closely to him. We formed a circle around him, and we were all crouching down in the bushes. He looked at each of us and said, "Listen carefully to what we are about to tell you. Courage, composure and caution are what we need.

Right now, we will be passing the most dangerous area on the back side of the mountain, right behind the Germans. They have observers everywhere. We will go down behind them and crawl on our stomachs so we don't become targets. The most dangerous spot is about five hundred meters ahead. Once we pass that area it will get easier. Be careful, and don't be afraid." He paused for a moment while we all huddled around him.

I looked over at my brother, and he looked at me; neither of us blinked, and we shared a deep breath.

The rebel continued, "If the Germans ambush us and shoot at us, we will shoot back. Each man has to watch out for his own survival. Listen to the password and the correct response. The password is *Leonidas*, and the response is *Dimos*. I will say *Leonidas* and you will say *Dimos*, then we should go." We took off one behind the other in a line.

By the time we reached the dangerous area it was completely dark. We dropped to the ground and crawled on our stomachs like turtles. We formed one line, and one behind the other, we crawled. I dug my elbows and knees into the dirt and pushed myself forward. Panayiotis was in front of me, and he would look back every few minutes to check where I was. I stayed right behind him.

Our stomachs rubbed against the ground for what felt like hours. The moon only gave us enough light to see what was directly in front of us. No one made a single sound. We passed right under their noses, unnoticed, thank God.

Around midnight, we reached a ravine and saw an old, tiny house near the edge. We went in and were told to sleep for a while. They assigned two of us at a time to stay up and keep watch in half hour shifts. When it was our turn, I held the gun and Panayiotis had the watch. The leader of the rebels spoke to us again and said, "If anyone shows up you say stop and if they don't stop, you fire." We both nodded at him.

We stood there near the door of the house. On the other side lay our comrades and in front of us there could have been anything. It was completely dark. As I stared off into the night, I began to remember all the times we would stay up studying together. We would struggle to see the letters and numbers under the candlelight. Those nights felt so distant in my memory, but here we were again, standing together through the night. Fortunately, no one came that night and no shots were fired.

Everyone woke up early the next morning and we got ready as quickly as possible. We walked all day, and by that afternoon we reached a village where we stayed for one more night of watching and guarding each other.

When we arrived at the Andarte camp where we stayed for two days, we were handed over to the military division. They received our credentials, and after they wrote down all our information, Panayiotis and I were taken, with a few other men, to a section of the camp for training. While we prepared for our training, they asked us to tell them what had happened to us.

We told them our entire story, and when we finished, they brought us to another section of the camp where we joined up with other men who had also been forced to wear German uniforms. All of us were sent to the town square where saw about seventy Serbians who had also been captives at Pavlou Mela. We recognized a number of them and while we were talking, one Serbian ran up to us. He was one of the men from Pavlou Mela who always shared his candy with us. He was ecstatic to see that we were alive.

These Serbs had also left the army camp and they had been fighting with the Andartes against the Germans. The brotherhood we developed with these men during our time in Pavlou Mela was incredible, so we formed a group of twenty-eight men—some of the Serbs and others of us who had been forced to wear German uniforms. We had one leader, Captain Aggelopoulos, who took care of us and trained us every day.

Our group began to work closely with the central headquarters of the Andartes that was located in the village where we were staying. After a few weeks in that camp, we were taken on a trip to repair roads in a neighboring village. We repaired these roads for ten days straight. When we returned, we continued our training as soldiers.

We trained physically and mentally, and we were preparing to take arms when we again told our superiors that we would be happy to do that once we reached our families. Captain Aggelopoulos agreed with this proposal. He loved all of us. He was with us every day, and over the weeks we were together, we developed a true friendship with him and the whole company became a family. He told us, "Hitler and his beasts will soon be finished. They do not fit into this land. They will be leaving shortly and our country will find peace." He would remind us of this on a daily basis, as we trained for the military while we worked in the camp. We were never inactive. If we were not repairing roads, we were chopping wood; there was always something to be done.

After a few more weeks, the day we had all been waiting for arrived. Captain Aggelopoulos approached us and said, "The Beast has begun to kneel. Things are clearer now more than ever, Hitler has been beaten." He looked at us, and I turned to my brother, his eyes shining with hope. Crowds filled the streets. We were all dancing along to a tune played from the violin we found. The tune was a melody of joy. Then the ringing of bells erupted under the gray sky and Greece was able to breath deeply again!

We marched back into Thessaloniki, the place where we had once been pushed down the streets as captives. This time, we walked down those same streets, but now people all around us rejoiced. An old man went to the top of a school's stairs and removed a Nazi flag from his pocket, nailed it to a piece of wood and lit it on fire. He yelled, "The wild dogs are gone!"

We walked throughout the villages around Thessaloniki. We journeyed back to Pavlou Mela to find that we had German captives in the same cells where we had been held. They were faced with the same cold steel and lonely solitude that they brought to Greece, but we did not torture them or starve them.

We stayed in Pavlou Mela for a week or so. On several occasions the Andarte officers stationed there insisted that we go back to headquarters in the mountains and we insisted that we must return home first. We assured them that we would take up arms and join the remaining resistance once we returned to our families. We told them out story again and again, and finally the Andartes gave in.

The day finally came when we would be able to leave and make our way home. Captain Aggelopoulos lined us up for the final time. There was my brother and me and the original group that had escaped together. One by one, he kissed us and gave us his blessings. He told us to remember all we had learned in our training, because that knowledge might prove to be useful. His last words to us were "Farewell, get home safely, and may God be with you."

We stood in a line staring at him for a moment until he turned around and walked away. We were given supplies by the Red Cross, and we were then sent off toward Kastoria.

***

Pappou allowed the notebook to slip between his legs and close of its own accord as it fell onto the floor. Pappou looked embarrassed as he murmured, "Sorry, Perry."

I reached over and picked up the precious notebook. "No problem," I said, a bit too heartily. I put the notebook in my bag. "Can I get you anything now?" I asked. He was obviously worn out and drained of any strength he had left.

"Maybe a little νερό ('water')," he nodded. Yiayia brightened. "Me too," she said.

When I went into the kitchen I found my aunt leaning against the counter, her arms wrapped across her chest, doing her best to hold her emotions deep inside of her, but not really doing a very good job of it. "We saw the doctor yesterday," she said. Her voice cracked as she spoke.

"What did he say?"

"She. The doctor. He's a she, a woman."

"Oh, sorry. Well, what did she say?"

My aunt jerked her head from side to side. "Can't you see for yourself?"

I nodded. "There's nothing more they can do?"

"No," she said, and then the quiet tears rolled down her cheeks and her body shivered slightly.

I reached out and put my arms around her. She allowed me to comfort her for a moment, but then she pulled away. My Aunt Barbara embodied what it meant to be a dutiful child and spent an enormous amount of time at my grandparents' house helping them. "You should give them their water," she said.

When I returned to pappou, he sipped his water slowly and gave his glass back to me. He looked a little better. I said, "How did you manage to crawl all that way on your stomach, just using your elbows to pull yourself forward? You must have been in agony."

"*Philotimo.*"

"Ok."

"I owed it to my brother, to the others. We all depended on each other. One mistake, we were all dead."

"No mistakes," said yiayia.

I was looking at him the way he appeared while we were talking that afternoon. Then I thought back to when I used to work with him and my dad when I was little. He was strong then. Powerful. He could have crawled on his stomach halfway across the Bronx.

"Perry," he said. "Help me get up."

I leaned over and placed his cane in one hand. Then I stood and supported his other arm. We walked very, very slowly together over to the window overlooking his garden, now all brown and withered by the cold and faint sun.

"Look over there," said my grandfather.

"Where?" I asked.

"There, in the corner next to the fence." He held up a skinny arm and pointed his bony finger.

I saw where he was pointing. A faint flash of red. Impossible, I thought to myself.

"The last tomato, Perry. Stubborn. It doesn't want to go." He gave me a small smile and looked at me. "But…it can't last much longer, can it, Perrymou?"

I didn't answer him. I simply looked at him and put my arm around his shoulders.

"Don't be sad," he said. "We've had this time together. You have my stories…and," he smiled. There was a slight twinkle in his eye, "there are a few more stories, Perry. Naí. We're not done yet."

"Good," I brightened up a little. "I'll see you next week, then."

I lingered at the house for a little while longer, but there wasn't much to talk about. Then pappou fell asleep on the couch, so I stood up to leave. That's when I noticed there were shirts and pants neatly folded on a chair next to the couch. On the floor under the chair were more blankets and two pillows. I realized the couch was where pappou was sleeping all the time. He didn't have the energy to walk to his room anymore.

The wind picked up as I walked out the door and down the street. Dark clouds rolled across the evening sky. The temperature dropped. I pulled the collar of my thin coat tightly around my neck. Just as I reached my car, the first snowflakes of winter began to fall.

CHAPTER 9

A Tempestuous History

*"Civil strife is as much a greater evil
than a concerted war effort as war itself is
worse than peace."*

—Heroditus,
Greek philosopher and historian.

Despite Greece's enormous cultural impact on Western civilization, it is a very small country that has been driven by "internal" wars since mythological antiquity. The Trojan War, triggered when Paris stole Helen from King Menelaus, is the background event for Homer's classic *Iliad* and his *Odyssey*, as well as Virgil's *Aeneid*—the three seminal texts of Western literature. Then there were the Peloponnesian Wars fought for over thirty years between Athens and Sparta, and the Athenian Civil War that broke out soon after the Peloponnesian Wars ended. Those wars were followed by various other clashes throughout Greek history, but they were all topped by the disastrous and terribly cruel Greek Civil War.

The most basic explanation for the civil war that broke out in late 1944, toward the end of World War II, as the Germans retreated from Greece, was that the conflict was a fierce struggle for control of the post-war Greek government between left-leaning, anti-royalist partisans who fought most effectively as guerilla fighters—the Andarte, the labor unions, the communists, the socialists and urban intellectuals who held the balance of power at the end of the German occupation, against the right-leaning, royalist, Greeks—privileged elites, the Orthodox Church, conservative villagers and peasants—who wanted the return of King George II. But in fact, the civil war was so prolonged and intense because it became the first proxy battle of the Cold War (1946–1991) between the Western Powers that supported the Greek right, and the Soviet Union that supported the Greek left. By the end of the Greek Civil War, at least 80,000 Greeks were killed in a bitter struggle that pitted brother against brother, fathers against sons and friends against each other.

So one might conclude that Greeks have more or less been fighting with each other since the dawn of their history. I have only seen and experienced this on a very small scale, and of course Greeks are not known for being calm. We often have a reputation for being stubborn or hard headed, which I certainly have a tendency to embody. I don't know that I necessarily believe that, but there have been times when my own life has been damaged by similar impulses, in other words, to argue with the people closest to me. There may be something in my Greek and Italian blood that makes me eager to defend what I think is right.

It certainly doesn't help that I think in terms of ideals and principles as a result of my study of philosophy. I have some understanding of what honor is, what dignity is and most importantly what duty is. I set standards for myself and others and do my best to stand by those ideas. These conflicts can sometimes occur regardless of who the other person is, and because my family is comprised of Greeks and Italians, and a number of my friends are as well, I can sometimes find myself in conflict with those around me.

Magnanimity, or turning the other cheek, has never been my strength. There are standards, and I adhere to them: If we are family, this is how we act. If we are friends this is how we act. If we are in a relationship, this is how we should act. If we love each other, we also have to respect each other and be honest with each other. If we don't disrespect each other and don't lie to each other, then we will all get along.

These simple statements have been the source of a considerable pain in my life because I abide by them fiercely and respond just as tenaciously when others don't. When one goes "all in" on love, family and friendship as I do, it is difficult to mitigate the urge to expect that others do the same. I have learned at this point in my life not to always express my opinion about what is best for others, and I do try to empathize with why others act as they do, but the bottom line is that "what is right, is right" and I will choose how I relate to others based on their actions. The best realization in this context has been to find the value in the principles themselves and the actions themselves without expecting reciprocation.

My occasional intensity is something my family members and friends have come to understand and respect. Nonetheless, it does sometimes separate me from other people. No one wants to be pressured to explain their actions when they are accused of being wrong and so best friends and family members have sometimes turned into my combatants as a result of my refusal to accept their behavior.

I can't help but think of my tempestuous history within my own world when reflecting on Greek history. From a very young age, I've tended to do and say what most try to avoid if I think it's the right thing to do. If there's a friend who forgets how to be respectful towards the group, I'm the one who gets in touch and has a sit down to remind that person. If there's a family member who forgets how to tell the truth, I will remind them. This puts me on the outs with other people, but I'm never on the outs with myself or my principles. Making choices and acting from principles or a sense of duty to others is how I operate. People may make promises they break, say things they don't mean and act in ways that I'll never understand, but I can understand ideals in myself and I can develop them easily and reliably. That is a price I am always willing to pay.

I think Plato's notion of the forms stuck with me in a unique way. When I read about his concept—that there's an ideal form of everything, I of course believed that we should strive for that perfection. Strive with me or move on is a mentality I have adopted. I have learned to not need perfection but believe that I should always strive for it. It's about the effort and the vision, not the result.

There is a phrase in our Italian Bari dialect, *Ce n'ge ma sci, sciamaninn, ce non gen a ma sci, non ge ne sim scenn.* Basically, it means, if we are going to go, let's go. If we are going to stay, let's stay. I have been awakened from many a deep slumber by my mother yelling "*Sciamaninn*" or "let's go." This small phrase is, of course, used for tasks like leaving the house, but it can also take on a more profound meaning: if you're going to do something, do it with passion, care and pride. If others don't abide by that, I have no business going anywhere with them. I've respectfully walked away from many things because of this short but powerful phrase. I have also learned how to do so more easily and give my all while expecting nothing in return. I now understand that the main motivation for doing something should not be the hope for reciprocation or acknowledgment, but the road to that realization has been a tough one.

Some recent issues were weighing heavily on my mind as I approached my pappou's house that December. Winter had finally arrived. The air was cold and damp from a heavy mist blowing in off Pelham Bay. I parked my car down the block, threw my bag around my shoulder and squinted into the cold air as I walked toward the house.

It was again my aunt who opened the door and hurried me inside to get out of the weather. I was pleasantly surprised at how energetic she was as she took my coat and hat and escorted me toward the living room. Then I heard her say, "Look who's come for a visit, pappou! It's Perry."

Yiayia was sitting in her chair and did not react to my aunt's voice. She was gazing at the television with a flat look on her face. I first walked over to her and touched her hand. She looked up and me with a smile and said, "Hi Bill." I kissed her on the cheek. She returned to vacantly gazing at the TV.

Pappou was lying on the couch, but he pulled himself up into a sitting position when I entered the room. He smiled when he saw me. "Ah, Perry. My grandson, the writer. Are you ready for more stories?"

"If you are, pappou."

"A few more, Perrymou, … a few. But, they are the most important ones."

"Why do you say that?"

"Endings are important, όχι?"

"Ναί, pappou, yes."

He was, if anything, even weaker and thinner than he was the last time I saw him, but his eyes still shined, and, as he began to speak, his voice was firm, if not strong. He looked up at yiayia to wave her over, but my aunt was standing behind my grandmother, nodding her head in opposition. "Ah, then we will let yiayia sit over there," he said with a soft voice. I went to pass him the notebook, but he shook his head softly to indicate he didn't need it. "Today, I will talk only from my memory, Perry, from my heart."

I nodded, and he began.

***

The Ninth Story:

When Panayiotis and I began our trip home, we departed from Kozani. Our destination was our village of Lagka just outside Kastoria. The roads were destroyed, and in general, everything was in ruins. We walked, one foot in front of the other, σιγά, σιγά, ("slowly, slowly"), spending our nights in different villages along the way. At various stops, our new friends we met during our march began to leave the larger group to return to their homes. Then, one morning, near noon, we passed by the willow tree where we were captured. We barely glanced at the tree. Soon, we were walking through the forests where we hid from the Germans, but we still kept on walking. Our stride never broke, even to eat. We were in a hurry to return to our family.

We finally reached Mt. Kryoneri, and we felt like we were almost home. We were getting close. When we approached Ondria, we reminded each other about when we had left from the opposite side of these mountains to arrive at the Andarte farm to get wheat, not knowing our search for food would lead to our sad adventures over the past year.

We continued to walk, and we could see that everything had been burned. All of our pyramid dwellings in the forest where the people from Lagka and other villages in the area had settled in the high mountains during the occupation had been destroyed. We passed the cave where we hid with our family, and there was not a soul in sight. My brother looked at me and said, "They must have gone back to the villages." He was right. We realized that when the beast had finally been expelled, our people hiding in the mountains had gone back to their homes. When we reached the edge of our village, the outskirts of Lagka, we saw that people had, in fact, returned and begun to rebuild their houses. We could see small stacks of wood and building materials, stone, bricks, tiles and glass piled around half-empty frames and the broken walls of shattered structures.

Despite our excitement, we calmly walked through the streets of our village, looking around, trying to see what had happened. Suddenly we heard a woman scream, "The kids are home!" We saw her run in the opposite direction, away from us, shouting, "The kids are home! The kids are home!" We still didn't run. We followed the shouting woman through the streets toward our old house, when suddenly we saw that our house had been burned to the ground, but we did not stop. Again we heard the cry, "The kids are home!"

We finally saw our parents. We stopped immediately and stared at them. My mother fainted and my father grabbed her as she fell. He wrapped his arms around our mother while he stared at us. His eyes were still shining blue but they were sunken deep in his face. It was our siblings who sprinted past our parents and embraced us. All five of them grabbed us, and we wrapped our arms around their heads as they buried them in our chests. We stood, without moving, totally still, and our feet finally rested beneath us. Our arms were around our family, and our heads were tilted toward the blue sky. I could hear the new wheat rustling in the breeze.

When we broke from our siblings, our mother caught her breath and our father was waiting for us, with his arms still wrapped around her. They both had tears running down their faces and our mother grabbed us and kissed our faces while our father hugged us. We sat this way for a few moments and then we began to really look around us at our village. So much of it was gone. Our mother held our hands and brought us to a neighbor's house where we sat at the kitchen table.

Our father sat across from us and told us that our house was totally destroyed and we would have to rebuild it. The very next morning we walked back up into the mountains that protected us during the bombings. My father,

Panayiotis and I started chopping trees and gathering stones. We prepared the materials, but we had no money to pay craftsmen since we had not harvested any corn or wheat to trade with them for their work, so we began the work ourselves. We did our best to prepare the foundation and as we worked our father reached an agreement with a contractor named Pandelis to help us.

As soon as we were ready to start building the foundation, Kosta, a distant relative and a neighbor of ours, came to the house. He said: "You don't have the right to build here. It is too close to the other houses. You have to move at least ½ meter to the right."

We were shocked. My father turned to him and said "Φύγε! ('go away'), Kosta. This doesn't concern you."

Kosta walked away, but two days later, we received notice that he filed a complaint against our family in the form of a lawsuit. When we confronted him, asking him why he did this, he said that the others in the village put him up to it. He gave us two names. These were the men who were tormenting the entire village, Vagios and Thanasis. They mounted accusations against people for false actions and brought them to the court, which was ruled over by the ruthless president of the court, a man named Gidarakos. People were even being exiled or killed. If there were informants willing to testify, regardless of how false the charges were, the accused could be brought before Gidarakos.

Our entire family was present in the court, but the inquiry focused on my mother, father, and Panayiotis. Gidarakos asked the informants, "What do you know that you want to bring before this court?"

One of the informants, Vagios, stood up and said, "I saw those three [my mother, father, and Panayiotis] hold and beat Kosta on his head."

My mother had a shocked look on her face. We all looked at each other in total disbelief. Vagios held out his shaking hand and pointed at my father. He kept talking and said, "Besides, Mr. President, he is also the uncle of the Rizopoulos who is a thief."

Vagios was referring to George Rizopoulos who was an officer in ELAS, the leftist organization that had lead most of the guerilla fighting against the Nazis.

Vagios's accusation that my father was somehow associated with the leftists was all that Gidarakos had to hear. Like most of the village at the time, Judge Gidarakos was a royalist who supported King George II. Actually, my father was also a devout royalist, but Gidarakos ignored our defense and punished us severely for the false charges that supposedly started over ½ meter of burned out land.

The penalty imposed by the court cost us roughly twice the cost of rebuilding our house. Panayiotis was sentenced to jail for a month, and my father was sentenced to 13 months in prison. Our friends and family helped us raise the bail money required to keep them out of prison. I walked out of the court with my brother, and I had the horrible feeling that all Greeks were turning on each other.

When we went home, we continued our work on the house. We gradually finished it, and Panayiotis and I found work in a nearby village where we earned enough wheat and other grain to pay for the rebuilding. However, we could feel that Lagka was being torn apart by the increase in court cases being brought before the ruthless Gidarakos. Neighbors began to look at each other differently. Our father told all of us boys not to get mixed up with the political infighting, and he encouraged Panayiotis and me to again go down to Argos for work. After we helped everyone move into the new house, both Panayiotis and I found jobs in a restaurant in a neighboring village.

But then the quarrelling in Lagka grew even worse. There was paranoia and mistrust in the hearts of everyone. Panayiotis and I continued to sleep in or new house while we worked in the restaurant and our younger brothers went to school. Then suddenly the troubles in our village boiled over.

Panayiotis and I were working when a police officer came into the restaurant asking for us. When we heard him, we scrambled out of the kitchen to meet with him, and he told us that our father had been detained under the suspicion that he was a communist.

We both ran out of the restaurant and went to see a man named Giannakis, our father's cousin. We knew that he worked for the king and was a member of the groups that had been taking people into court and accusing them of treason. He told us, "Boys, they have taken your father away in order to exile him. You need to rush to find Konstantinos, the attorney, so he can work with the court to stop the proceedings. If you don't, your father will be tried as a traitor and sent to Makronisos." Makronisos was a barren, deserted island where the royalist courts were sending anyone who they believed to be a communist to be tortured and often executed.

I yelled at Giannakis, "What did you do when they took him away? What did you say?"

Panayiotis was also yelling, "What are you talking about? Do you believe that our father is a criminal?"

Giannakis said nothing. He just looked at us and hung his head in shame. When his father wanted to marry my father's sister, my father, the man

Giannakis had just allowed to be arrested, helped him pay for the wedding and gave him two gold pounds.

Panayiotis continued his harangue of Giannakis. "So this is the thanks we get? Leave us alone and get out of our way!"

We soon found out that our father was taken along with two other men to the prison in Kastoria. The King was sending out groups of soldiers to round up the communists throughout Greece, and both of those men arrested with our father were actually known communists.

Meanwhile, a number of the King's men were coming to eat in our restaurant. We befriended some of them and a few were men from our area who knew our family. We spoke to them and explained our situation. They, of course, knew that our father was a Royalist and that the charges against him were not true. They assured us that they would find a way to get him out of jail.

It took a few days and we finally got word that our father was released. He came to the restaurant where our boss prepared a meal for him. We all sat and tried to celebrate when Panayiotis suddenly saw one of the men who was responsible for arresting our father. We both went outside to confront him. He saw us coming and began to walk away. I yelled to him and he stopped about 40 feet away from us. He yelled back at us, "What do you want? Your father was released."

Panayiotis yelled back, "All will answer to God for their acts."

The traitor walked away and we went back to sit with our father. He looked at the both of us and said, "Don't worry, my children. God will pay them back, don't try to get revenge. It will only make things worse for us."

We both quietly looked at him and then said, "Okay."

* * *

Pappou's voice when he finished his story was barely a whisper. Yiayia reached over toward him. He held onto her hand. She had a half smile on her face that reflected both concern and confusion. It was a difficult moment for the three of us.

"Pappou," I spoke gently, "are you alright?"

"Naí, Perrymou, … yes … yes." He spoke slowly. "I am very sad."

"What about?" I feared the answer.

"Greece. My country. The hatred we had for each other when there was so much need for love."

"Oh, I can understand that." I said, somewhat relieved he wasn't talking about himself.

"How could we go through so much pain and suffering under the occupation," he paused, breathing slowly, "and then start killing each other?"

"I don't know," I said. "I don't understand this part of Greek history."

"Don't you?" he said. He raised his head slowly and stared me down. I gave a slight smile before his steady gaze. "We Greeks are like a family," he added.

"Pappou…" I stammered.

"I know you very well."

"You do."

He ignored me. "You have the best and the worst things from all of us," he said.

I cracked another half-smile. "I know what you are telling me."

"You have to learn how to calm down." He raised his hands and widened his eyes. He clutched his fists and shook his hands slightly. "Too much."

"But…

Pappou sighed and tapped my leg. He turned toward yiayia. "*Philotimo*," he said. Her gaze remained unbroken. I could see and feel the impact her lack of responsiveness had on him.

I looked him in the eye and then looked only a couple of feet over his shoulder. Sitting on a small table to his left was a vase from Greece. It was another portrayal of Achilles sitting with Patroclus and they were sharpening their weapons. That vase had been sitting in that spot for as long as I could remember. He noticed that I was looking in that direction.

"You can't always be like that. It's not good, Perrymou."

"I know."

Expecting this unwavering answer, he gave way to a slight smile "Maybe when you find the right woman."

"I'm working on it," I responded with a smile.

"I need to go to the bathroom," said pappou. "Will you help me, Perry?"

"Of course," I said.

I helped him off the couch. More by picking him up than anything else. He was light as a feather. As I placed his feet on the floor, I was afraid he would fall, but he was steady, and after a few seconds he was able to straighten himself. He placed one arm around my waist, and I placed one arm around his waist. We walked together as I supported him as we walked together across the room.

I brought him to the door and opened it. He did what he had to do, quietly, without complaint. He opened the door, and I could see it was a struggle to stand. I grabbed him again and we walked together back to the couch.

"That was *philotimo*," he said with a smile.

I would like to feel that I understood immediately what he meant, but I didn't. Not really, although I had some sense that he was saying I acted out of caring and respect to help someone I loved. And in retrospect, that may have been all that he meant. To act out of love and caring. To show my best to the world even in difficult situations.

My grandfather leaned back into the couch. "I need to rest, Perry."

"Do you want me to stay for a while?"

"If you want. To keep yiayia company." He stretched himself out along the couch and I covered him with a blanket. "Σε αγαπώ (I love you)," I said, but he had already fallen asleep.

CHAPTER 10

The Irrational Universe

"The source from which existing things derive their existence is also that to which they return at their destruction."
—The Milesian Greek philosopher Anaximander, *(610–c. 546 BCE) the author of the first surviving lines of Western philosophy.*

I spend a lot of time, maybe too much time, trying to understand what it means to be Greek and American, or Italian and American. My friends and I often gather at a café in Astoria, Queens. It's our location for trying to make sense of our lives. There's a common stereotype of old Greek men sitting in cafes talking and arguing through the day into the evening. In Astoria, one is just as likely to find groups of young people talking and arguing, but the purpose of our group is the same as it is for the groups of old men: We support each other and help each other sort out the day-to-day problems that complicate our lives. It's a very Greek thing to do. We sit for hours talking, eating or just drinking alcohol or frappe.

Not all of the people in my group are Greek. There's the "Not Greek" Nick, James, Dave, and a few others. But the rest of us are Greek, or at least, like me, partly Greek. The "Greek" Nick and Georgia are far more Greek than I am, both are fluent in the language and make frequent visits to Greece and Cyprus. All of us balance each other out, and we pick each other up when one of us has a problem. We share the spirit of *philotimo*.

One of our on-going discussions centers around the question I am trying to understand—what makes those of us who are Greek different from other young Americans, or sometimes the question is phrased, are we really all that different? I know that I feel different, but is that because I really am, or because I want to feel that I am different to maintain my allegiance to my vision of my pappou? Also, in all honesty, I even feel different from Greek-Americans my age. I don't speak the language very well, I went to public school and not parochial school, and I don't visit Greece.

All that considered, my non-Greek friends would agree that the Greeks, myself included, are generally more intense. All the other non-Greeks are way more lighthearted and easy going. They would also all agree that I'm the most intense of the guys, and Georgia, a Cypriot immigrant, is the most intense of the girls.

One evening I told my friends that I had asked one of the classes I teach, "What is the first thing you think of when you hear the word 'Greek'?" They all said, "Yogurt!"

Everyone around the table laughed.

A peripheral friend, a Greek-American said, "But there's also Bakalava, Spanakopita, Moussaka."

I interrupted him, "Those are all still food. Be better."

Everyone laughed again.

Then I said, "Alexander the Great and Hellenism, there are cities that still bear his name. There's Democracy, Philosophy, Medicine, the Olympics, c'mon, bro."

"Greeks haven't done much since ancient times though," he said.

At this point my friends saw me winding up. It was ironic because everyone else at the table was "more Greek" than I am, but I'm often the most vocal in conversations like those.

"Not true," I said, "during WWII we stalled the Nazis on their way to Russia, but I won't go into detail on that. What about George Stephanopolous, Maria Callas, Bob Costas, Arianna Huffington…"

"And John Stamos," said Georgia with a grin.

"We can't forget about John!" I said with a smile.

On a somewhat more serious note, I gradually became aware that only the Greeks among my friends, work with their parents in businesses their parents own. Georgia is very intelligent and a radiation therapist who also works at her family's diner in Brooklyn. I am currently an adjunct philosophy professor, but I often work at my father's real estate office. Another friend, Taso, owns a deli with his brother. Even John Stamos worked at his family's diner before he became famous, as the story goes. The Greek entrepreneurial spirit is one way we've been successful in this country, and my father has often warned me not to let our businesses fall apart. He'll say things like, "If I drop dead you have to handle this."

Whenever our group talks about work, we invariably end up talking about our families, which then invariably leads to talking about relationships. As Freud said, work and love. When we work with our families, those elements mix and they can get explosive.

When you're born Greek, marriage is an expectation.

One of our friends, Nicole, just left a three-year relationship. She told us: "My yiayia called me the other day and asked if I was dating anyone. I said, 'Not seriously, I'm dating to see what's out there, but I haven't met anybody yet.' All my yiayia said was, 'Don't be too free because people will talk.'"

"Ok, thanks, yiayia," said Georgia.

We all understood where her yiayia was coming from.

"Wow, that's some village stuff," added the "Greek" Nick.

Every spring we talk about plans to go to Greece or Cyprus for a few weeks in the summer. I often talk about pappou's stories and his fond memories of Greece despite what he experienced during WWII. But I don't really need to convince anyone. My friends really love Greece.

"Things are totally different there," says Georgia.

Everyone nods in agreement.

"It can get up to 115 degrees. But you're never uncomfortable."

"Yea," Nick adds, "it's a dry heat so it's great. You don't even feel the heat."

Georgia continues in rhapsody: "It's gorgeous, you get off the plane and the air is just different. Everything tastes better. Drinks tastes sweeter, the fruit is better, everything is better."

We sound just like the old guys reminiscing at other tables around us.

It's the same with politics. Often, instead of arguing about US politics, we argue about Greece—the devastated economy, the failure of both the Socialists and the Conservatives, German bullying, the EU, Turkey's occupation of a part of Cyprus. We often rant about Turkey. Georgia's family was directly impacted by the conflict in the 70's. This along with conversations with my good Armenian friend, Paul, have led me to make sure that I teach my students about the Armenian Genocide. When we talk about Cyprus, we talk about Turkey and to talk about Turkey without talking about what happened in 1915 would be impossible, at least if I'm there. As the government does not officially acknowledge this genocide, it is important that I tell my Ethics classes about how memory, truth, and identity are all connected in the present with our actions. As such, I always take the wheel for this part of the discussion, but we all rant rather often about Armenians and Greeks. We all agree that as Greeks, we're similar to Armenians.

I usually include a few facts and then try to prevent myself from dominating the conversation too much. "Well, when the Ottoman Empire broke up, 1.5 million Armenians were slaughtered by the Turks. God knows how many Greeks." I raise my eyebrows and say, "Αυτή είναι η αλήθεια! ('That's the truth!')"

We have also launched, from those tables, a number of half-baked ideas to save the world. Recently, the "Not Greek" Nick and I mapped out an idea for a non-profit on a napkin over burgers and frappe. The idea was actually very good, but we know we'll never follow up on it. Still, we have fun working on these ideas. Most of the time they are well-meaning distractions. We've saved the world at least five times at the café. I think that I can't have a bad idea while drinking frappe.

I guess our conversations aren't truly particularly "Greek." They're very normal discussions by young people trying to figure out their lives. Most of us have been in and out of relationships, switched jobs or had tough times at jobs. We've all been struggling with work and love over the past couple years which, as Freud put it, are the cornerstones of our humanness.

I was recently teaching a course where I integrated Existentialism and Absurdism, and at the end of one class, on Friday, I wrote on the blackboard, "The universe is meaningless and irrational." Then under that I wrote, "Have a good weekend." My students had a moment of contemplation, and then left for the weekend with a smile. Afterwards, I thought to myself, is that what it means to be Greek? Is that what it means to be human? We are simply making up all this meaning?

The following day, as I often do, I took that profound question to the Long Island City Piers with me for a jog. I had a quick stretch and started jogging along the water, moving and pondering. I ran until my feet hurt, then kept running and kept thinking. I ran until I was drenched in sweat and leaned up against the railing for a second. I ran until my lungs begged me to stop and until a rush of calm came over me. The next day was Sunday and I knew I was going over to pappou's house. I knew our story was getting towards the end and that it was time to prepare.

Even when pappou's health was truly failing, he was still encouraging me. He continued with his 'you're the best' line, and it's crazy to me that even at the worst of times, on death's doorstep, that's all he wanted to tell me. Even then, he didn't talk about himself. The focus was on me feeling good about myself and moving forward with confidence.

I remember our last story-telling session. We were sitting on the couch and I had my arm around his back. He was in considerable pain when he grabbed my hand on his shoulder and repeated that phrase, "You're the best, Perrymou." Then he struggled into his last story.

***

The Tenth Story:

Finally the time had come for us to move into our new house with our whole family. Panayiotis and I were still working at the restaurant in Argos, so we managed to help the family and maintain ourselves with the salary we received. For a while, it looked like life was getting better, but it wasn't.

In late 1946, the King's soldiers in our area were often fighting against guerilla elements of armed Andartes and communists. Once again, we heard the hiss of gunfire and the explosion of mortars around us. And then the funerals began, dozens per day for the soldiers who were dying in hospitals. Mt. Malimadi, outside of Kastoria, would light up each night with gunfire. The public school in our village became a hospital for Kastoria, and the mountain was covered with dead bodies.

Soldiers from two of the King's battalions, the 74th and the 75th, would often come by our restaurant. We watched their numbers dwindle every time they came in to eat. The Andartes had gained strength and they were armed just as heavily as the King's soldiers. And this was a very different war then the one fighting against the German occupation. This time both groups knew how to fight in the mountains. We were all children of Greece, and we used our birthright to our own destruction.

One day in the restaurant there was a group of men wearing the King's uniform sitting in a corner. One of them, a lieutenant, was crying uncontrollably as he sat and held his face in his hands. Although we did not know these men by name, when one of the soldiers left the table, I approached him and asked why the lieutenant was so upset. He told me that they just killed a group of Andartes who were firing machine guns from a camouflaged nest. They had them cornered, and the man crying ran close enough to throw a grenade. He killed the Andartes and saved his comrades lives, but when they went to identify the bodies, the dead men were unrecognizable. The lieutenant went through their remains to find their identification cards. When he found the first card, he dropped to his knees. It was his brother's card. I looked toward the lieutenant again and he was holding the identification card pressed to his face as he cried.

A few days later we received news that the King's soldiers were going to seize my grandfather's land, the land of my grandfather on my mother's side. Again, someone had run to the local government and told them that my grandfather was a communist so they seized his property.

My grandfather had purchased that land; it was not an inherited lot. When he died, his land would become ours. The government represented my grandfather as a captain of the guerilla group ELAS and a communist. He was 81 years old, but they designated him, along with two other men, as communists. It was true that both of these other men were openly communist, but again, my grandfather was a royalist. It didn't matter. A decision was reached, and within hours all of his properties were seized. The government wanted the land around our village and this was a perfect way to achieve their aim. Once again, Panayiotis and I had to spend the little money we had to hire a lawyer to fight this verdict. Luckily, we found a good lawyer who was able to get the land unbound.

So we were totally out of money at this point. What could we do? Every few weeks it was something new. They had taken family members as prisoners, almost exiled my father to his death and now they were trying to take away our means of survival. I had to do something or they would keep attacking us until someone was killed. I decided, after they tried to take the land, to join the army and fight for the King. I assumed that if my mother and father were willing to risk one of their sons to fight for them, they would leave us alone. I went to the army headquarters in Kastoria. They gave me my uniform, I filled out identification paperwork, and I became a soldier in the King's army.

On one of our first missions, we marched into a small, sleepy village in Macedonia. We were sent there to ensure that there was no communist activity, but there didn't seem to be any military activity at all. Myself and the other men in my unit, there were about fourteen of us total, marched through this village. There were a few people in the town square. When they saw us, they all went into their homes, except for one old man who remained seated on a bench. We walked through the town, fanning out in pairs.

I'd only walked a few steps when I heard screams. Quickly, my partner and I made our way back to the square. We saw the old man on the bench being choked by one of our soldiers. The soldier had the strap of his gun wrapped around the man's neck, and he was twisting his gun to turn the strap on itself and choke the old man. The other soldier was casually lighting a cigarette. I ran over and asked them what the old man had done.

"Don't worry about it! He's a Bulgarian," the smoker shouted.

I yelled at him, "If he isn't guilty of anything, let him go!"

The man with the cigarette in his mouth started laughing. The old man was gasping for air. People heard our yelling and peered out of their windows to see what was happening.

A man around my age came running toward us and yelling. He was pleading with us to let the old man go. He did not get close to us, because he didn't want to look like a threat. The man with the cigarette pointed his gun at the man. He stopped and raised his hands, still pleading.

"He is my father," he said. "He hasn't done anything, please let him go."

The soldier placed his knee on his father's back and pulled the strap, just like the Germans did to us. I remembered my uncle being beaten in the square. I yelled at the man again, "He is just an old man, let him go!" I lunged at the soldier and grabbed the strap to loosen it from the man's neck. When I did this, the soldier I had been walking with did the same, and we freed the old man. His son immediately ran up, grabbed his father and they went back to their home.

The father was an unarmed, innocent old man and two of my fellow soldiers would've killed him. Those soldiers were doing the same thing to other Greeks that the Nazis did to them and their families. And the smoke from one soldier's cigarette reminded me of the Nazis burning our villages and playing cards as the smoke rose into the sky. How could my own people do this?

My unit moved around a lot, and we fought in many areas of Greece. I was almost killed three times. Two of the times were in the Battle at Florina. I wrote to Panayiotis after that battle because I, myself, was shocked that I survived.

The Florina district is in the northwest, near the borders with Albania and Macedonia, that was controlled by leftists for most of the civil war. The guerillas were secured in good positions on the sides of the mountains. We knew that it would be very dangerous to take their positions and get them out of the district because we had no choice but to charge their positions and hope to overwhelm them. That would mean facing machine gun fire like Panayiotis and I had faced from the Germans when we were captured during World War II.

When we approached the enemy in the foothills, they began firing even before we tried to climb into the mountains. My heart was racing as they fired down on us, and I began to return fire in their direction. As we were running into position, they began launching grenades at us. As I was running, a grenade landed only two feet away from me. I dropped to the ground, and all I saw were the insides of my eyelids. The grenade didn't go off, and I did not stop to check it or try to find out why.

When I opened my eyes, I ran to join the other soldiers who had established a position. We were on one knee, using the houses as cover, in an attempt to return fire and move forward. We ran between houses and made our way through the village. I was running with a few men by my side, and as we were about to enter a house I heard one of them yell, "Get down!" I jumped to the ground and rolled away from the house and a bomb destroyed the house that we were about to enter. The roof collapsed, and I looked to my side and saw it crumble.

We fought through the village returning fire and eventually we made it to the foot of the mountain. We had the guerillas outnumbered and that day they had to flee through the mountains out of Greece. These were Greeks driven out of their own country because of politics.

When Panayiotis wrote me back, he was shocked that I came so close to getting killed. He said that God was watching out for me.

The next time I barely survived was in Karditsa. It was another village, similar to Florina because it was near mountains. The battle there was vicious. Again, we were fighting to get into positions on the mountain.

The fighting took place between the houses. We would get into a safe position, take aim, fire, and then move if our position was taking too much fire. The idea was to always move forward and force the enemy to retreat.

We were resting one night in the village and I was cooking in a house we occupied. I did a lot of cooking during my time in the military because that was the trade I brought with me and so they used me quite often. I even did a great deal of cooking for some of the higher military officials. One night they let me have liquor and that was the first time I ever got drunk. I drank until I couldn't see straight, and then I vomited when I was walking back to our sleeping area. I also started smoking during the war. These were things that happened because of the stress, especially after the early battles when I saw the results of war.

I was preparing a dinner that night in Karditsa, and all of a sudden I heard gunshots close by. I was used to hearing gunshots in the distance, almost constantly, but these were very close. I was only armed with a handgun, but I took cover and took my gun out. I stayed low and made my way across the house. I poked my head out from the window, and I could see people approaching and firing. I put my hand over the windowsill and fired back, as did the other soldiers by my side.

I needed to make a run for my rifle. When I got to the door, I made the sign of the cross and burst through the doorway. I made a quick left and ran as fast as I could. I felt the air was hot with gunfire, and I could feel bullets whizzing by me. I ran down the small streets of the town as the walls around me were being pummeled with bullets. Unbelievably, I made it to our quarters where there were other soldiers scrambling to arm themselves.

When I went to grab my gun and get bullets, my hand grazed against my coat. I looked down, and there were bullet holes in the sides of my coat. The bullets had grazed my sides, but there was no blood. I again made the sign of the cross to thank God for my good fortune, and followed the other men out to fight.

After the civil war ended in the fall of 1949, I continued to work in restaurants for a few years, but I knew I had to leave. The civil war inflicted even more damage on Greece, and we had already suffered in World War II. At least 80,000 people were killed and over 70,000 were left homeless. And there was still a lot of hatred and suspicion in our villages. I knew I had to go to America. I didn't want to leave everyone. I knew I would miss my mother, my father, Panayiotis, and all my brothers, but I felt that I had to leave.

Most of the village came to see me off. All of my family members and some of our closest friends even came to the port. I kissed and hugged each and every one of them goodbye. I was wearing a suit my father made for me. I had a suitcase with a few pieces of clothing, and I had $37.00 in my pocket. I also had a small notebook with a few names and addresses of people I could count on when I arrived in New York, people from Kastoria. And I did have a job lined up with a man named Christos at a restaurant called *Neo Zoe*, or "New Life" in Manhattan.

I boarded the boat. I stood along the railing and waved goodbye to my family. I looked at Panayiotis, and we both gave each other a small nod and a smile. I looked at my mother, and she smiled and waved as tears ran down her cheeks. I looked back at them until I couldn't see them anymore, and then I tuned away.

I looked up at the sun and it shined on my face. I closed my eyes, and I could feel everything we had been through. My heart began racing, and I tried to take a deep breath but I couldn't. I felt paralyzed. It was only the sound of the waves that brought me peace. It was only the sound of the waves that reminded me of the good times, and I remembered as I always did, the wheat songs that were placed so long ago in our hearts by my mother as we worked in the fields.

* * *

When my pappou finished, he still tried to sing his wheat songs the way he had when he first told me the story when I was a child. His eyes were wide open and he swung his arms back and forth with a smile, but he could not muster the strength to sing anymore. He had his wheat songs, but they were trapped inside him when he handed me the notebook for the final time.

That night I had a dream that I was with my family and we were driving around in our car. Pappou flew into the car and then flew out. Then a butterfly flew into the car. I cupped it in my hands and released it out the car window. Then another butterfly flew into the car and I tried to capture it, but I couldn't. I woke up from that dream in the middle of the night, and I knew that something was wrong. The following morning, pappou went into the hospital. He did not make it out.

I texted all my friends and asked them, "Café at 7:00?" They all came. They knew I had something important to tell them, so they were there for me at the café. We sat and made small talk until the food came and before we started eating, I told them that pappou died. They all consoled me and said they would be at the wake. I thanked them and found myself going through the motions, calmly telling my friends the horrible story of his dying.

Pappou's wake was filled with people who knew him, from members of his church congregation to people from the neighborhood, people he worked with decades ago, and people who saw him at his desk in my father's office just days before he died. He was a number of things to a number of people, but very few people knew the details of his life—the events that shaped the man.

His brother, Dimitri, came from Long Island with his entire family. My pappou and Dimitri were the only two brothers who came to America, and they were very close. Dimitri did know the events that shaped the man. During the wake he pulled me close to him and said, "Perry, you have his name." I hugged Dimitri and replied with a smile and a simple, "I know."

One of the most difficult things about my grandfather's death was that he had to go without yiayia by his side. A few days before he passed, during his last stay in the hospital, I was sitting in his house visiting with yiayia while my aunt stepped out for a breather. My mother was visiting pappou in the hospital, and so, using our cell phones, we created a video chat between pappou and yiayia.

When pappou saw yiayia on my mom's phone, his face lit up, although he was very weak. He smiled when yiayia said, "Σ 'αγαπώ πολύ, Περικλής," or "I love you very much, Pericles." They exchanged a few more smiles and waves and then we had to stop our chat. When we hung up, yiayia turned to me and said, "He's a good man. He'll be home soon." I nodded and held her hand.

When my father came home from the hospital with the news that pappou had died, before he even sat down, or even before anyone could console him, he looked up and asked, "How am I supposed to tell my mother?"

The next few days passed in a fog. The pain of losing him was mixed with the banality of our rituals associated with death. Putting on a suit, shaking hands of acquaintances offering condolences, paying the funeral parlor, a man from Greece taking pictures of the body for his brothers back in Kastoria who could not make it. It's almost inspiring how numb we can make ourselves when there are things to be done.

There were a few moments of genuine feeling and commemoration of this man amidst the perfunctory declarations. A cousin, Louis, who is a Greek-Orthodox Priest, gave a warm speech about pappou. Pappou had been so very proud of Louis when he became a priest, and Louis remembered that. He stood in front of the full room in the funeral parlor and delivered a speech about the *agapi* pappou had. *Agapi* is a Greek word, uniquely Greek in its definition. Unlike English, Greek has different kinds of love. *Agapi* is a pure, spiritual kind of love. For Louis and for everyone else in that room, that is the kind of love pappou expressed for all of us. Louis's speech was greeted with a warm applause, and I gained a great deal of respect for him that night.

Louis's speech truly set in during the funeral service. All four of us, my father, mother, sister, and I sat in the front row of Zoodohos Peghe. My father's sister, Barbara, sat next to me, and my sister's boyfriend, sat between her and my mother who was with my father the whole day. I held my Aunt and she sobbed for the majority of the service. My gaze was locked on the altar, and I felt a cold focus come over me only moments into the start of the service. I stared blankly at the altar and my mind was fixated on the idea of *agapi*, and what that meant to me. I sat, stood, and walked, but barely felt like I was there. I knew that this was not it, this was not his end.

My father was brought to the front of the church and he put pappou's necklace that commemorated his membership in the Archons, a lay religious fraternity dedicated to working for the Orthodox Church, around his own neck.

The priest said many nice words about pappou and reminded the congregation of all that he gave to the church in which we sat. There were so many gifts. We all walked up to the casket and paid our final respects. I helped my Aunt from the front of the church back to her seat and then out of the church to the limo. The limo began its trip to the cemetery.

After speaking to three doctors and countless family members and friends, we decided that it would be best to not have yiayia at the services although my father made sure the hearse drove by their house. I like to imagine that she was sitting in her chair and felt him smile at her for the last time as we drove by. We made our way through the Bronx until we reached the gate of the cemetery. I remembered that I had been to visit Giuseppe a few times at another cemetery. I would go sometimes and talk or write to him.

It was a beautiful day and the sun shined as we all exited the limo and everyone walked from their cars to the burial site. Father Sylvester said some final words over the casket. I looked up at the sun behind him. For a moment there was a slight breeze. The flowers around the casket swayed. I looked to my sides and saw my family calmly standing by each other.

Father Sylvester finished his words. My Great Uncle Dmitri looked at me. He placed his flower on the casket, walked over to me and put his hand on my shoulder. We looked at each other for a moment. His eyes are bright blue like pappou's. With his hand on my shoulder, we exchanged a nod and he walked away. That single nod was an agreement. There was no need to say anything, in that moment, we both knew it was up to me, when that casket drops, to not let pappou down. That is the freedom and the burden on my name and position as the only male in my generation from his side of the family.

The day after the funeral, we all went to yiayia's house to deliver the news. We greeted her, and I sat on the couch in the usual spot where pappou and I had our final talks. My sister, Christina, sat next to me. My mother and father stood near yiayia and my dad kneeled down next to her as she was sitting in her chair and he told her "Ma, dad passed away yesterday." She looked up at him and said, "He's still in the hospital."

"No, mom," said my father, "he passed away yesterday."

Yiayia looked up at my father, blankly, and she began sobbing. Christina and I left the couch, and all the family stood around yiayia touching her shoulders and hands. She started crying more intensely and saying, "He is such a good man." We all agreed and didn't leave her side until she calmed down a bit.

Then my mother grabbed a napkin to wipe yiayia's eyes. Christina started crying, so I put my arm around her. We sat in silence for a few minutes with the television playing in the background. Suddenly yiayia looked at Christina and saw that my sister's eyes were red. Yiayia asked her, "What's wrong?" We all looked at each other and said nothing. Yiayia continued, "Where's my husband? He's still in the hospital, no?" We all looked at my father as he leaned in again and said, "Yeah, mom, he's in the hospital. Say a prayer for him."

Yiayia made the sign of the cross, and started watching television. To this day, she still thinks he's in the hospital. We protected her with dignity, and we did the best we could. She no longer goes to our church, Zoodohos Peghe, because everyone would only want to talk about pappou.

Since pappou's passing, I can still hear him telling me, "You must replace me now, Perrymou." That was the last thing he said to me.

For months I carried his words in my heart as a burden. Even now, I have yet to allow my sadness to wash over me because I force myself to stay strong just as he would have stayed strong, and, if I am supposed to replace him, then I must stay strong. But of course I cannot replace him. Not really.

Epilogue:
A Bright White Light

"Tell me, O muse, of that ingenious hero
who travelled far and wide..."
—*The opening lines of 'The Odyssey,' an*
epic poem by Homer, circa 900 BCE.

Not long after pappou died, I was at my uncle Dimitri's house on Long Island, and I found myself staring at a photograph of pappou as a young man just as he was ready to leave Greece and begin his new life in America. I must have seen the photo many times before, but on that occasion, the picture compelled me to think about why this quintessentially Greek man would, or even *could*, leave Greece to begin a new journey in America. It was obviously too late to ask pappou, and I had no notebook to guide me toward an answer. Perhaps for the first time, I understood that I was on my own if I wanted to understand what drove my grandfather to make that journey that changed his life and, ultimately, gave me my life.

***

The Untold Story:

As horrible as World War II and the Nazi occupation had been for Greece, there was, by all accounts, more suffering and there were more deaths during the Greek Civil War than during the German/ Italian occupation. This post-World War II situation was pretty much unique to Greece because, rather than falling quickly into either the Soviet or the American spheres of influence, Greece became the first victim of the Cold War. And while other countries were able to begin their process of postwar rebuilding, Greece was involved in a process of bitter postwar destruction that lasted over four years, from mid-1944 until 1949. There were assassinations, pitched battles, betrayals, murders, deportations, and mass killings on both the left and the right sides of the conflict that resulted in starvation, financial ruin and dislocations for significant amounts of the civilian population even if they were not directly involved in the conflict. Furthermore, just as my pappou had told me, the worst fighting, the most egregious reprisals and the greatest suffering occurred in the mountain areas of central Greece where the ebb and flow of the war meant that villages passed back and forth from the control of either the communist-led left or the royalist-led right. And it was the villagers who paid the price.

Although the battles were theoretically fought on ideological grounds, practical, down-to-earth men like my pappou often became involved for practical, down-to-earth reasons. I remembered that he told me that although his family was sympathetic to the democratic, leftist forces, and some of his family even fought with the communists against the Nazis, it became necessary for my grandfather, in order to protect his immediate family, to join up and fight for the king's army because those were the people who held the most power in his particular village. If he didn't fight for the king, his family would have been destroyed.

However, it must have also become obvious to my grandfather that protecting his family from the fighting was only the first step in the survival of his mother, his father and his six other brothers. Even when the civil war finally ended, there was no money, no commerce, very little food and replanting the war-ravaged land was difficult. There were no "wheat songs" sung in the fields during those tough times, and there was always the possibility that despite the truce of 1949 that ended the civil war, fighting could break out again at any moment because of the remaining terrible animosity between the two sides.

And so emigration from Greece became a practical alternative for men like my pappou, and the most desirable destination was the "magical" land of America. (Although Greece remains a relatively small country of 11 million or so, there are over 5.5 million Greeks living in other countries—over three million in the United States.) He was always the breadwinner for his family, and once he arrived here, despite his own initial poverty and his determination to build a life with my yiayia, there were, according to my conversations with Uncle Dimitri, a steady flow of payments from pappou back to the family in Greece. Those cash flows made it possible for the family to not only survive, but also to succeed. All of the younger brothers became educated and they all eventually held good jobs in Greece as teachers or government officials.

But my heart tells me that there was another side to my pappou, to that practical, hard-working man, that also contributed to his decision to come to America. It was the ancient siren song calling Greeks to passion and adventure, to living out their own individual sense of *philotimo*. In my grand-father's case, it was the same willingness to risk his life that drove him and Panayiotis to recklessly attempt to gather wheat for their family during the war. It was the same willingness to take risks that drove him to join the king's army despite the great dangers he would face. And it was that same romantic ability to take a risk that drove him to America. It was, in a sense, the memory of the wheat songs and the wind rustling through the grain—his personal siren song—that gave him the strength and courage to always move forward and honor his Greek soul.

Dimitri also told me that no one in the family forced pappou to leave Greece. No one even suggested it. His mother and his brother, Panayiotis, actu-ally opposed my grandfather's emigration, and they begged him to stay with the family. Dimitri agreed that the times were especially difficult in postwar Greece, but he also felt that the family would have muddled through and survived just as they had for so many previous generations. "Your pappou was a dreamer," said Dimitri. "Most people only saw the side of him that was a strong-willed, very responsible man who took care of his family, but he was also a dreamer who would not stop until he made his dreams come true." He took my hand and looked me in the eye. "You are so much like him, Perry." Then he repeated his admonition from the funeral: "That's why you must be the one to honor his name." Then he hugged me and kissed me on the cheek.

***

A few weeks after the funeral, I had a dream that I was an old man. I was sitting in a white lawn chair in a yard full of bright green grass. My arms and legs ached. I was tired, half dozing, as I watched my grandchildren roll and wrestle in the grass a few yards away from me. I felt happy. Then I looked up at the sun. As my gaze lingered, the sun grew bigger and brighter. I was unable to turn away, and when I continued to gaze into the sky, my entire vision was consumed by a bright, white light. There was a dull buzzing sound that grew increasingly louder and sharper, and then suddenly I was jolted awake.

There was no lawn chair. There were no grandchildren. There was no light. In fact, it was still early morning and quite dark. I sat for a moment at the edge of my bed as my crucifix and *corno* dangled from my chest, swinging in the breeze from my ceiling fan. I took a few deep breaths, I dressed, walked out to my car and drove to our old neighborhood in the Bronx. The first gray and pink light of dawn filtered through the naked branches of the trees that lined the deserted, chilly streets. I passed by my family's old semi-attached home, by Giuseppe's and my grandmother Elizabeth's house, pappou's house, the avenue we spent hours walking up and down when I was a child and drove up and down Pelham Parkway.

I drove in the gathering rush hour traffic across Fordham Road into northern Manhattan, Inwood, past our old stores where the sidewalks were filling up with adults hurrying off to work and kids shuffling slowly toward school as the pale winter sun rose over the gray buildings and shuttered storefronts. I opened my driver's side window and felt the cold air in my face the way it felt when I walked the streets with pappou and my dad, two grown men and their little man going off to work.

Then I circled around and headed back against the commuter traffic, back into the Bronx. Eventually I found myself outside Zoodohos Peghe church, under the familiar steeples topped by Byzantine crosses. I parked and entered the church through a side door. I made my sign of the cross and knelt in a pew near the altar. The weak sunlight straining through the windows just barely lit the intricate carvings on the polished wood. A few sputtering candles flickered off to my right. I tried to concentrate, tried to remember how excited my grandfather was when he saw the completed altar for the first time.

Still, I must admit I didn't find the solace I was seeking in the empty church. The memories of pappou's funeral were too recent, and I was still shaken after the dramatic confusion of my "sun" dream. I sat for a while anyway, staring at the altar, the icons and the murals, hoping my anxiety would calm. It didn't, so I slipped back outside.

I got back in the car and drove over the Triborough Bridge into Queens. I drove until I reached the piers at Long Island City. I parked a couple blocks away from the water and began walking. It was still cold and the wind picked up, blowing wet off the water. I stood there looking out over the water, watching it sway in the gentle motion from the waves. It was dusk and the lights from the Manhattan skyline glistened off the ocean. I rested my elbows on the top of the fence that lines the edge of the pier. It was bitterly cold as the wind whipped across my face. I stood there, just breathing, staring into the water. I felt my foot begin to bounce up and down, I started walking along the pier. I kept my eyes on the waves as I walked.

I started to hear my father say, "He wants to know if you're made of ashes." I smiled to myself.

I kept walking into the cold air and a slight smile continued on my face. I looked up at the tall apartment buildings and back across the water. I came to the end of the pier and reached into my jacket pocket and grabbed my *komboloi*. I twisted the beads around my palm and rested by forearms on the railing and gazed out at the waves as they moved under the moonlight. I could still hear pappou's voice in my head. I could hear his questions, his encouragement and his memories.

A few days later, I ran into my cousin, Saki, who had noticed me studying the picture of my grandfather getting ready to leave Greece. He had, unknown to me, made a copy of that photo and he gave it to me. I put it in my pocket and later, at the café in Astoria, I showed it to my friends. We made our usual route down 30th Avenue and down to Athens Square Park. We all sat on a bench near the statue of Sophocles and the ancient Greek styled pillars of the park. I took the picture out. I passed it to Dave and Georgia.

"He looks a little like you," said Georgia. "He must have been about the same age you are now."

"Yeah, a little older" I said.

"When he came to America?"

"Yeah," I said as I leaned back on the bench, locked my fingers and put my hands between my chest and my stomach. I looked to my left and saw a statue of Sophocles and then around the small park to gaze at the statues of other great Greek Philosophers. I had spent hours on top of hours studying Plato, Aristotle and the others; reading, writing, thinking and interpreting their work and there they stood in front me frozen in stone. It's how we choose to live that keeps them alive. Their memory is not in the finely shaped stone, but in the hands that thought it a worthwhile task to erect the statues. That is what keeps their ideas alive. It is only what we, as people, do that counts and how we constantly bear the freedom and responsibility we have as people to create meaning.

We are always faced with the resounding question of how to live well. The answer to this call is always in our hands, our minds and our hearts and once we are aware of this, it is never far away. A great man who faced insurmountable evil with unyielding courage and belief, and a man who meant a great deal to me, had passed away. As I sat and talked with my friends, I had one rhetorical question on my mind. Who am I? I am his grandson, and more importantly I am still alive and completely aware that I was blessed to walk alongside him.

I decided that I was not simply another person who had known him, loved him and only would remember him with my thoughts and an occasional story.

I would do and keep doing until I couldn't. This story would be one of the things I would hold on to, craft and share. This would be a way I could choose to stand for goodness. I wanted to do nothing more than to work.

I still miss him. But as time passes, I have only been emboldened by the obligation that I am blessed to carry our story. I am thankful for our love and only strengthened by the loss. Losing pappou has been one of the greatest pains in my life thus far and has been the single thing that has given me the most strength. I made strength from this pain and purpose from his passing.

As Camus said, "I only know of one duty, and that is, to love." To choose to love, to fight and to create and not grieve in the face of loss is the courage my pappou inspired and the actions that he deserves. I am empowered by our shared *philotimo*. That is the gift he left me. The meaning we make in this life is always ours and I promise to live my life with tired hands.

Index

CPSIA information can be obtained
at www.ICGtesting.com
Printed in the USA
BVHW03s2146241018
531024BV00014B/44/P

9 781618 117724